DeepSeek and Mental Health Support Among Chinese Youth

This book examines the impact of the AI tool DeepSeek on mental health care in China, offering valuable insights into challenges, ethical considerations, and the transformative potential of AI.

Co-authored by a clinical psychologist and an AI expert, it explores the mental health crisis among young people in China, including societal pressures, cultural norms, and systemic barriers. This book provides a balanced analysis of the limitations and benefits of AI-driven, round-the-clock assistance, while addressing ethical concerns and presenting future research directions to navigate emerging challenges at the intersection of technology and mental health.

Enriched by compelling case studies, this title is essential for those interested in the evolving relationship between AI and emotional well being.

DeepSeek and Mental Health Support Among Chinese Youth

Use Cases, Risks, and Broader Implications

Olive K. L. Woo and Yuk Ming Tang

CRC Press
Taylor & Francis Group
Boca Raton London New York

CRC Press is an imprint of the
Taylor & Francis Group, an **informa** business

First edition published 2026
by CRC Press
2385 NW Executive Center Drive, Suite 320, Boca Raton FL 33431

and by CRC Press
4 Park Square, Milton Park, Abingdon, Oxon, OX14 4RN

CRC Press is an imprint of Taylor & Francis Group, LLC

ISBN: 978-1-041-09244-5 (hbk)
ISBN: 978-1-041-09245-2 (pbk)
ISBN: 978-1-003-64913-7 (ebk)

DOI: 10.1201/9781003649137

Typeset in Sabon
by SPi Technologies India Pvt Ltd (Straive)

This book is dedicated to all those seeking hope and healing in their mental health journey, and to the innovators working tirelessly to make care accessible to everyone.

Contents

About the Authors

Dr. Olive K. L. Woo, PsyD, is a licensed clinical psychologist with over a decade of clinical experiences in public settings. She is recognised as an associate fellow in Hong Kong Psychological Society and a fellow in Thanatology with the Association of Death Education and Counselling in the U.S.A. Olive has been serving as an honorary clinical supervisor at both the University of Hong Kong and the Chinese University of Hong Kong. Olive is the author of the two guidebooks, *Artificial Intelligence in Cognitive Behavioral Therapy: A Guide for Mental Health Professionals* and *Virtual Reality Interventions for Patients under Palliative Care: A Practical Guide for Healthcare Professionals*. She is also the founder of the evidence-based psychological intervention titled *Flourishing-Life-Of-Wish-Virtual Reality Therapy* (FLOW-VRT®).

Dr. Yuk Ming Tang received the B.Eng., M.Phil., and Ph.D. degrees from the Chinese University of Hong Kong, Hong Kong, in 2000, 2003, and 2007, respectively. Following his graduation, he worked as a post-doctoral fellow with the Faculty of Medicine, CUHK. He is currently a senior lecturer with the Department of Industrial and Systems Engineering, the Hong Kong Polytechnic University, Hong Kong. He has published more than 80 articles in internationally refereed journals, including numerous contributions to top-ranked publications. His research interests encompass artificial intelligence (AI), virtual reality (VR), the Internet of Things, digital twin technology, blockchain, and sustainable technology within Industry 4.0, as well as healthcare applications. Dr. Tang serves as the lab-in-charge and is a key member of several laboratories and Joint Research Centres focused on the development of projects involving AI and other advanced technologies.

Contributor bio

Dr. M. W. Geda is a project fellow at the Hong Kong Polytechnic University. He earned his Ph.D. in 2021 from the Department of Industrial and Systems Engineering at the Hong Kong Polytechnic University. He also holds a master's degree in Industrial Engineering and Management from Politecnico di Torino, Italy, and a B.Sc. in Industrial Engineering from Mekelle University, Ethiopia, where he graduated with honours. Dr. Geda has a extensive experience in academia and research. Previously, he served as a postdoctoral fellow at the Laboratory for Artificial Intelligence in Design (AidLab) and as a research fellow in the Department of Industrial and Systems Engineering at the Hong Kong Polytechnic University. While at AidLab, he led a research project on Big Data analytics for product and service design. Dr. Geda has published in reputable journals, including the *Journal of Industrial Information Integration*, *Journal of Intelligent Manufacturing*, and *Engineering Applications of Artificial Intelligence*, among others. His research interests span human-centred design, human-computer interaction (HCI), applied computing, and artificial intelligence.

Preface

The emotional well-being of young people in China is in crisis. Overwhelmed by academic pressures, economic uncertainty, and cultural expectations, many grapple with anxiety, depression, and other mental health challenges. Yet, societal stigma and a severe shortage of professional mental health resources leave countless individuals without the support they desperately need. In this context, technology offers a glimmer of hope. The rise of artificial intelligence (AI) has opened new possibilities, providing accessible, stigma-free, and culturally sensitive solutions. However, integrating AI into mental health care brings both opportunities and challenges, demanding careful attention and caution to ensure its safe and responsible use.

At the forefront of this revolution is DeepSeek, a groundbreaking Chinese AI platform that has captured the attention of millions. Unlike traditional mental health services, DeepSeek combines advanced natural language processing, emotional intelligence, and cultural customisation to deliver empathetic and meaningful support. For many, it has become a trusted companion, offering solace and guidance in moments of distress. With its ability to address mental health challenges at scale, DeepSeek represents a transformative shift in how emotional care can be delivered in a society where seeking help has long been taboo.

This book explores the intersection of DeepSeek, mental health, and technology, examining the cultural, social, and technological factors that have shaped its rise. The first section examines the mental health crisis in China, highlighting barriers such as stigma, structural challenges, and cultural norms that prevent young people from seeking help. The second section explores how AI, through platforms like DeepSeek, addresses these issues by leveraging cutting-edge technology to provide tailored mental health support, with case studies illustrating its impact on individuals' lives. The third section considers the broader implications of AI in mental health care, emphasising the need for ethical frameworks, robust policies, and regulations to ensure its safe and responsible use.

This book is not just about technology—it is about people. It is about the students, young professionals, and everyday individuals finding hope and healing through AI in a society that has long struggled to discuss mental health. It is about the potential of technology to bridge the gap between need and access, offering a new path forward for emotional well-being, provided it is implemented with care and responsibility. However, without careful oversight, it also carries significant ethical and psychological risks. Through its story, we explore the possibilities, limitations, and future of AI-powered mental health support—not just in China, but around the world.

Acknowledgements

We would like to extend our heartfelt gratitude to the many individuals who have contributed to the creation of this book.

First and foremost, our deepest thanks to our contributor, Dr. M. W. Geda, for his significant contributions to the three chapters specifically focused on DeepSeek, which greatly enriched the content and perspective of this work.

A special thank you goes to Ms. Hoi Man Au and Ms. Tsz Yan Tam for their diligent efforts in assisting with the literature search.

We would also like to express our sincere appreciation to the reviewers whose insightful comments and constructive feedback helped strengthen the manuscript.

To everyone who has supported this project in ways big and small, we are sincerely appreciative. This book is the result of a collective effort, and we are truly grateful for the contributions of each and every one of you.

Part 1

The mental health crisis in China

Chapter 1

The silence crisis: Overview of mental health challenges among young people in China

Olive K. L. Woo

INTRODUCTION

In recent years, mental health issues among young people in China have become a growing concern, often referred to as a "silence crisis" due to the stigma and limited open discussions. Despite the country's rapid socioeconomic development, the psychological well-being of its younger generations remains precarious, with increasing rates of anxiety, depression, and other mental health disorders. This chapter begins with the prevalence of mental health issues, followed by an exploration of the multifaceted nature of this crisis, examining the cultural, familial, social, and economic factors that contribute to the mental health challenges faced by Chinese youth.

The mental health crisis

Mental health challenges have become an alarming public health concern in China, especially among adolescents and young adults. Despite China's substantial progress in many domains, mental health remains a relatively neglected topic, with many young people facing psychological distress without adequate support or intervention. Epidemiological data highlight the severity of this crisis.

Studies of meta-analyses estimate the prevalence of depression symptoms among Chinese adolescents ranges around 20% or higher, while anxiety symptoms affect a substantial proportion of this population (Zhou et al., 2023a, 2023b). Suicide has emerged as a leading cause of death among Chinese youth aged 15–24, with recent trends showing an alarming increase in suicide rates among adolescents since 2017 (Hu, 2023; Yang, 2024; Yang et al., 2025).

DOI: 10.1201/9781003649137-2

Specifically, suicide rates among urban Chinese adolescents aged 15–20 nearly doubled between 2017 and 2021 (Yang, 2024).

CONTRIBUTING FACTORS

The mental health crisis among young adults in China arises from a complex interplay of cultural, societal, and economic factors, which together leads to the mental health crisis among young adults in China.

Cultural norms and stigma

In Chinese society, mental illness is often stigmatised and viewed as a personal or familial failing, tied to the concept of "losing face." This stigma may have discouraged young adults from seeking help, leading to internalisation of distress. Studies confirm that Chinese youth often conceal mental health struggles to avoid shame and protect family reputation, consistent with Confucian values emphasising filial piety and collective honour (Zhang et al., 2023). The taboo surrounding mental health has been compounded by societal expectations of stoicism and resilience, which further suppress open communication about emotional difficulties (Yang, 2024). The stigma associated with mental illness aggravates this problem, as many young adults may feel reluctant to seek help due to fear of social judgement or family shame, further reducing service utilisation (The Lancet, 2024).

Family expectations and socioeconomic influences

Family dynamics also play a critical role. Parental educational expectations affect adolescents' mental health, with higher parental pressure linked to increased depressive symptoms and suicidal ideation (Yang, 2024). The one-child policy generation faces unique burdens, as single children often bear sole responsibility for elderly care, which may intensify psychological stress (Zhang et al., 2023). In addition, socioeconomic factors such as parental education, income inequality, and urban-rural disparities may lead to mental health disparities. Research shows that urban environments are associated with higher rates of mental health issues compared to rural areas, due to factors such as noise, reduced social cohesion, and increased cost of living (Buttazzoni et al., 2022). Adolescents from lower socioeconomic backgrounds or rural areas experience higher rates of depression and anxiety, partly due to limited access to mental health resources and educational opportunities (Yang, 2024; Zhang et al., 2023).

Academic pressure

Another prominent contributor is the immense academic pressure faced by young people in China. The highly competitive education system, centred around the *gaokao* (national college entrance examination), imposes significant stress from an early age. This examination system fosters a culture where students' self-worth is heavily tied to academic performance, generating intense stress, anxiety, and burnout. Empirical studies reveal that approximately 65% of *gaokao* students report anxiety, with high rates of depression, sleep disturbances, and burnout (Fu, 2024). A study conducted by Wang and Fan (2023) in Jiangsu province finds that academic stress directly impairs sleep quality, with anxiety and school burnout serving as mediating factors, highlighting the psychological toll of prolonged academic demands. Although school-based psychological programmes are associated with improved mental well-being, many schools still lack sufficient psychological support. In addition, the intense focus on academic success often leaves little room for emotional development (Zhang et al., 2023).

Career pressure and unemployment

The pressure does not abate after the *gaokao*; university graduates face fierce competition in the job market, with pressure securing employment amid rising youth unemployment rates exceeding 20% (Tan et al., 2024; Zhang et al., 2023). Despite overall economic growth, studies reveal a paradoxical decline in youth confidence about future development, linked to widening income gaps and social inequalities (Anders et al., 2023; Haselbach et al., 2025; Park et al., 2021). Evidence indicates that perceived income inequality among peers is associated with poorer mental health outcomes, lower self-esteem, and increased interpersonal difficulties among adolescents, independently of objective family income (Schoon & Henseke, 2022). This erosion of optimism contributes to feelings of helplessness and mental health vulnerability, as young people from disadvantaged socioeconomic backgrounds are at higher risk for mental health problems.

Phenomena such as "involution" (excessive competition with diminishing returns) and "lying flat" (withdrawal from societal pressures) reflect young people's psychological responses to these socioeconomic challenges. Peer-reviewed studies have documented that involution and lying flat are prevalent coping strategies among Chinese youth in response to fierce social competition and pressure (Zhu et al., 2025). While involution involves investing more time and effort in competition, often without satisfactory outcomes, lying flat represents a conscious withdrawal from such competition, which may provide short-term relief but is associated with increased fatigue, anxiety, and problematic behaviours like excessive smartphone use (Zhu et al., 2025). The adoption of these strategies is closely linked to the broader context of career-related stress, which has been shown to correlate with depressive symptoms and feelings of guilt, particularly during the transition from education to employment (LaMontagne et al., 2024; Tang et al., 2024). Among unemployed young people in China, the prevalence of depression is near 50%, highlighting the severity of the issue (Hua & Ma, 2022).

Economic uncertainty

Economic instability exacerbates psychological distress among young adults in China. Despite the nation's rapid economic growth, many youths face soaring living costs, unaffordable housing, and unemployment (Tan et al., 2024; Wang & Tapia Granados, 2019). Peer-reviewed research consistently links financial stress to increased feelings of inadequacy and hopelessness, both of which are established risk factors for depression and anxiety. For example, a study examining Chinese adolescents finds that perceived family financial stress is closely associated with depression, particularly symptoms such as hopelessness and worthlessness, and could even increase the risk of suicidal ideation and self-injury (Yang et al., 2023). Evidence from a large-scale national survey indicates that indebtedness acts as a chronic stressor, negatively impacting mental health and increasing the risk of mental disorders among Chinese adults (Liu & Zhang, 2024).

Impact of social media

Digitalisation and the widespread use of social media have increasingly influenced mental health outcomes. Peer-reviewed research consistently demonstrates that while digital platforms can foster social support and connectivity, excessive or problematic use is associated with a range of adverse mental health effects. High social media usage has been linked to increased risks of depression, anxiety, psychological distress, and loneliness, particularly among adolescents and young adults (Khalaf et al., 2023; Naslund et al., 2020). Systematic reviews and meta-analyses consistently show that frequent engagement with multiple social media platforms correlates with more symptoms of depression and suicidal ideation (Naslund et al., 2020). The mechanisms underlying these effects include social comparison, cyberbullying, and fear of missing out, all of which can exacerbate feelings of inadequacy, low self-esteem, and psychological distress (Khalaf et al., 2023; Peprah et al., 2024; Ursula, 2024). Cyberbullying, in particular, has been shown to significantly increase the risk of sadness, anxiety, and psychosomatic complaints among teenagers (Khalaf et al., 2023; Peprah et al., 2024). Alarmingly, suicide rates among Chinese adolescents have increased in recent years despite previous declines, with academic pressure and bullying identified as key triggers (Yang, 2024).

Impact of the COVID-19 pandemic

The COVID-19 pandemic has a profound and lasting impact on young adults' mental health. Prolonged school closures and shifts to online learning disrupted academic progress and social connections, increasing feelings of loneliness and disengagement (Wang et al., 2020). A longitudinal study shows that depression and anxiety rates among Chinese adolescents rise significantly during and after the pandemic's peak, with contributing factors including reduced physical activity, increased screen time, and family conflicts during lockdowns (Wang et al., 2020). University students experience heightened mental health symptoms linked to quarantine, lifestyle changes, and uncertainty about career prospects (Wang et al., 2025). In addition, economic uncertainty and job insecurity during and after the pandemic have led to heightened career anxiety and psychological distress among university students and recent graduates (Gao & Li, 2024; Zhou et al., 2022).

Limited professional support

Despite the prevalence of mental health conditions among young adults in China, there remains a shortage and uneven distribution of mental health resources and professionals. There are approximately two psychiatrists per 100,000 people, a figure that remains far below the global average and insufficient to meet the population's needs (Xiang et al., 2018). There is also a shortage of child psychiatrists, with fewer than 500 child psychiatrists in the whole country (Wu & Pan, 2019). The shortage extends beyond psychiatrists to other essential mental health workers such as clinical psychologists, social workers, and occupational therapists. China has roughly 5,000 clinical psychologists nationwide, a stark contrast to countries like the United States, which has about 200,000 psychologists for a much smaller population (Fang et al., 2020). The scarcity of trained professionals in community and primary care settings further limits early intervention and ongoing treatment, reinforcing a predominantly biomedical model that emphasises hospital-based care over community integration (Xiang et al., 2018).

Besides, most professionals are concentrated in urban psychiatric hospitals, leaving rural areas severely underserved (Xu et al., 2018; Yan & Tu, 2023). The numbers of mental health staff in some regions, especially poorer regions of China, are even lower than those in many lower-middle-income countries (World Health Organization, 2021). This urban-rural disparity means that at least half of China's population who lives in rural areas may have limited access and utilisation of basic mental health services. The uneven distribution of mental health professionals is largely due to the healthcare budget being disproportionately skewed towards the urban areas (Xiang et al., 2018; Yan & Tu, 2023). Despite recent national reforms aiming to expand mental health services, including the establishment of mental health clinics in every prefecture-level city by 2025 and the promotion of a unified mental health hotline, disparities persist (Xinhua, 2025; Reuters, 2025). Rural populations face challenges such as fewer specialised clinics, limited availability of trained professionals, and inadequate referral systems linking schools and communities to mental health care (He & Wu, 2025; Wang, 2024). Study also highlights that young adults in rural areas often prefer initial mental healthcare options that are community-based and accessible, underscoring the need for tailored service delivery models to bridge urban-rural divides (Zhang et al., 2025). In small-sized and mid-sized cities, there are no full-time psychiatrists who specialise in treating young people, making specialised care inaccessible (Sun et al., 2024). Only a small fraction of mental health professionals offer psychotherapy, with merely 6.9% being clinical psychologists and 5.0% being counsellors (Yue et al., 2022).

Together with the high financial costs, psychotherapy is still mostly out of reach (Shi et al., 2020). This issue is exacerbated by the lack of medical insurance coverage, leaving the individuals to pay the full cost of treatment such as in community rehabilitation services (Ding et al., 2022). In short, the government has placed ongoing efforts on integrating mental health services into primary healthcare facilities and rural areas; however, access and quality of care remain uneven (China Daily, 2025; Fan et al., 2022). Without affordable care options, many individuals forgo treatment, leading to untreated or misdiagnosed conditions that worsen over time (Yang, 2024).

CONCLUSIONS

The mental health crisis among Chinese youth, often described as a "silent crisis," underscores a critical public health challenge requiring urgent attention. The rising prevalence of mental health conditions among young people highlights the need for innovative strategies to address this multifaceted issue. Cultural stigmas, academic and career pressures, economic disparities, and social media influence have been identified as factors leading to the psychological struggles faced by this demographic. In the next chapter, we will explore the deep-rooted stigma and barriers that may have prevented the young generations from seeking help, laying the foundation for later chapters, where the role of AI as a mental health companion can step in.

REFERENCES

Anders, J., Jerrim, J., & Macmillan, L. (2023). Socio-economic inequality in young people's financial capabilities. *British Journal of Educational Studies*, *71*(6), 609–635. https://doi.org/10.1080/00071005.2023.2195478

Buttazzoni, A., Doherty, S., & Minaker, L. (2022). How do urban environments affect young people's mental health? A novel conceptual framework to bridge public health, planning, and neurourbanism. *Public Health Reports (Washington, D.C: 1974)*, *137*(1), 48–61. https://doi.org/10.1177/0033354920982088

China Daily. (2025, January 3). Pediatric, mental health services to be expanded. https://www.chinadaily.com.cn/a/202501/03/WS677734e5a310f1265a1d8baf.html

Ding, R., Zhu, D., Wang, Y., Yong, M., Shi, X., & He, P. (2022). Medical service utilisation and direct medical cost of depression: a cross-sectional analysis of urban medical claims data from China. *BMJ Open*, *12*(9), e056422. https://doi.org/10.1136/bmjopen-2021-056422

Fan, X., Zhang, W., Guo, Y., Cai, J., & Xie, B. (2022). Equity assessment of the distribution of mental health beds in China: based on longitudinal data from 2011 to 2020. *BMC health services research*, *22*(1), 1453. https://doi.org/10.1186/s12913-022-08658-z

Fang, M., Hu, S. X., & Hall, B. J. (2020). A mental health workforce crisis in China: A pre-existing treatment gap coping with the COVID-19 pandemic challenges. *Asian Journal of Psychiatry*, *54*, 102265. https://doi.org/10.1016/j.ajp.2020.102265

Fu, Y. (2024). The impact of Gaokao high-stakes testing on student mental health in China: An analysis of stress levels and coping mechanisms among senior high school students. *Research and Advances in Education*, *3*(5), 23–32. https://www.paradigmpress.org/rae/article/view/1136

Gao, Z. H., & Li, J. (2024). Intolerance of uncertainty and mental health in China "Post-pandemic" age: The mediating role of difficulties in emotion regulation. *PLoS One*, *19*(2), e0298044. https://doi.org/10.1371/journal.pone.0298044

Haselbach, F., Mehlig, K., Friberg, P., & Chen, Y. (2025). Impact of neighborhood income inequality on adolescents' mental health. Results from the STARS study. *Health & Place*, *91*, 103391. https://doi.org/10.1016/j.healthplace.2024.103391

He, Q., & Wu, Y. (2025, May 14). Scroll locked: Why rural teens in China struggle to disconnect. https://www.sixthtone.com/news/1017085/scroll-locked:-why-rural-teens-in-china-struggle-to-disconnect

Hu, G. (2023). *Suicide Prevention: More Actions Are Needed*. China CDC Weekly. https://weekly.chinacdc.cn/fileCCDCW/journal/img/cover/0e30450b-f4c5-4394-9ac4-e06ae01235aa.pdf

Hua, Z., & Ma, D. (2022). Depression and perceived social support among unemployed youths in China: Investigating the roles of emotion-regulation difficulties and self-efficacy. *International Journal of Environmental Research and Public Health*, *19*(8), 4676. https://doi.org/10.3390/ijerph19084676

Khalaf, A. M., Alubied, A. A., Khalaf, A. M., & Rifaey, A. A. (2023). The impact of social media on the mental health of adolescents and young adults: A systematic review. *Cureus*, *15*(8), e42990. https://doi.org/10.7759/cureus.42990

LaMontagne, A. D., Too, L. S., Witt, K., Evans-Whipp, T., Owen, P. J., & Toumbourou, J. W. (2024). Does adolescent depression modify the association between psychosocial job stressors and mental health in emergent adulthood?. *American Journal of Industrial Medicine*, *67*(1), 44–54. https://doi.org/10.1002/ajim.23547

Liu, J., & Zhang, Y. (2024). Indebtedness and mental health in China: The moderating roles of income and social support. *Frontiers in Public Health*, *11*, 1279683–1279683. https://doi.org/10.3389/fpubh.2023.1279683

Naslund, J. A., Bondre, A., Torous, J., & Aschbrenner, K. A. (2020). Social media and mental health: Benefits, risks, and opportunities for research and practice. *Journal of Technology in Behavioral Science*, *5*(3), 245–257. https://doi.org/10.1007/s41347-020-00134-x

Park, L. E., Jung, H. Y., Lee, K. S., Ward, D. E., Piff, P. K., Whillans, A. V., & Naragon-Gainey, K. (2021). Psychological pathways linking income inequality in adolescence to well-being in adulthood. *Self and Identity*, *20*(8), 982–1014. https://doi.org/10.1080/15298868.2020.1796777

Peprah, P., Oduro, M. S., Atta-Osei, G. et al. (2024) Problematic social media use mediates the effect of cyberbullying victimisation on psychosomatic complaints in adolescents. *Scientific Reports*, 14, 9773. https://doi.org/10.1038/s41598-024-59509-2

Reuters. (2025, April 7). China expands mental health services to narrow gaps. https://hrone.com/blog/china-expands-mental-health-services-to-narrow-gaps-reuters

Schoon, I., & Henseke, G. (2022). Social inequalities in young people's mental distress during the COVID-19 pandemic: Do psychosocial resource factors matter?. *Frontiers in Public Health*, *10*, 820270. https://doi.org/10.3389/fpubh.2022.820270

Shi, W., Shen, Z., Wang, S., & Hall, B. J. (2020). Barriers to Professional Mental Health Help-Seeking Among Chinese Adults: A Systematic Review. *Frontiers in psychiatry*, *11*, 442. https://doi.org/10.3389/fpsyt.2020.00442

Sun, M., Zhou, H., Li, Y., Wang, J., Yang, W., Gong, Y., ... & Zhou, L. (2024). Professional characteristics, numbers, distribution and training of China's mental health workforce from 2000 to 2020: A scoping review. *The Lancet Regional Health–Western Pacific*, *45*, Article 100992. https://doi.org/10.1016/j.lanwpc.2023.100992

Tan, M., Wu, Z., Li, J., Liang, Y., & Lv, W. (2024). Analyzing the impact of unemployment on mental health among Chinese university graduates: A study of emotional and linguistic patterns on Weibo. *Frontiers in Public Health*, *12*, 1337859. https://doi.org/10.3389/fpubh.2024.1337859

Tang, Q., Lei, G., Zhang, Y., & Shi, H. (2024). The relation between mental health and career-related stress among prospective graduates in higher education stage during the COVID-19 pandemic: An evidence based on network analysis. *Frontiers in Psychology*, *15*, 1381846. https://doi.org/10.3389/fpsyg.2024.1381846

The Lancet. (2024). Helping young people thrive in China: Policy and culture. *The Lancet (British Edition)*, *403*(10436), 1513–1513. https://doi.org/10.1016/S0140-6736(24)00809-2

Ursula, B. (2024). Social media and mental health: Exploring the impact of digital connectivity. *Global Media Journal*, *22*(69), 1–4.

Wang, C., Pan, R., Wan, X., Tan, Y., Xu, L., Ho, C. S., & Ho, R. C. (2020). Immediate psychological responses and associated factors during the initial stage of the 2019 coronavirus disease (COVID-19) epidemic among the general population in China. *International Journal of Environmental Research and Public Health*, *17*(5), 1729. https://doi.org/10.3390/ijerph17051729

Wang, H., & Fan, X. (2023). Academic stress and sleep quality among Chinese adolescents: Chain mediating effects of anxiety and school burnout. *International Journal of Environmental Research and Public Health*, *20*(3), 2219. https://doi.org/10.3390/ijerph20032219

Wang, Q., & Tapia Granados, J. A. (2019). Economic growth and mental health in 21st century China. *Social Science & Medicine (1982)*, *220*, 387–395. https://doi.org/10.1016/j.socscimed.2018.11.031

Wang, Y. & Tan, G., & Zhu, T. (2025). The changes, formation and public policy measures of mental health in Chinese youth. *Frontiers in Psychology 16*. https://doi.org/10.3389/fpsyg.2025.1583594

Wang, Z. (2024). Bridging the gap: Challenges to mental health education for rural left-behind children in China. https://lkyspp.nus.edu.sg/gia/article/bridging-the-gap-challenges-to-mental-health-education-for-rural-left-behind-children-in-china

World Health Organization. (2021). *Mental health Atlas 2020*. Geneva: World Health Organization.

Wu, J. L., & Pan, J. (2019). The scarcity of child psychiatrists in China. *The Lancet Psychiatry*, *6*(4), 286–287.

Xiang, Y. T., Ng, C. H., Yu, X., & Wang, G. (2018). Rethinking progress and challenges of mental health care in China. *World Psychiatry: Official Journal of the World Psychiatric Association (WPA)*, *17*(2), 231–232.

Xinhua. (2025, March 10). China to expand mental health services nationwide. http://english.scio.gov.cn/m/pressroom/2025-03/10/content_117757145.html

Xu, J., Wang, J., King, M., Liu, R., Yu, F., Xing, J., Su, L., & Lu, M. (2018). Rural-urban disparities in the utilization of mental health inpatient services in China: The role of health insurance. *International Journal of Health Economics and Management*, *18*(4), 377–393. https://doi.org/10.1007/s10754-018-9238-z

Yan, Y., & Tu, Y. (2023). The impact of China's urban and rural economic revitalization on the utilization of mental health inpatient services. *Frontiers in Public Health*, *10*, 1043666–1043666. https://doi.org/10.3389/fpubh.2022.1043666

Yang, C. (2024). Research on China's adolescent mental health policies – Analysis based on PMC index model. *Frontiers in Public Health*, *12*, 1408991. https://doi.org/10.3389/fpubh.2024.1408991

Yang, Q., Zhang, W., Wu, H., Huang, B., Zhang, C., & Niu, G. (2023). The association between perceived family financial stress and adolescent suicide ideation: A moderated mediation model. *Behavioral Sciences (Basel, Switzerland)*, *13*(11), 948. https://doi.org/10.3390/bs13110948

Yang, R., Zhou, J., Bigambo, F. M., Yan, W., Wang, X., & Yang, H. (2025). The trend of suicide and self-harm in the Chinese population from 2018 to 2022 based on ambulance medical emergency cases: A retrospective study. *Frontiers in Public Health*, *13*, 1494841. https://doi.org/10.3389/fpubh.2025.1494841

Yue, J. L., Li, N., Que, J. Y., Hu, S. F., Xiong, N. N., Deng, J. H., … & Sun, H. Q. (2022). Workforce situation of the Chinese mental health care system: Results from a cross-sectional study. *BMC Psychiatry*, *22*(1), 562.

Zhang, P., Yang, F., Huang, N., Yan, W., Zhang, B., Zhang, C., Peng, K., & Guo, J. (2023). Assessment of factors associated with mental well-being among Chinese youths at individual, school, and province levels. *JAMA Network Open*, *6*(7), e2324025. https://doi.org/10.1001/jamanetworkopen.2023.24025

Zhang, W., Li, H., & Chen, Y. (2025). Choice preferences for mental health services among young adults in rural China: A discrete choice experiment. *Journal of Psychiatric Research*, 154, 123–131. https://www.sciencedirect.com/science/article/pii/S0190740925001501

Zhou, K., Chen, J., Huang, C., & Tang, S. (2023a). Prevalence of and factors influencing depression and anxiety among Chinese adolescents: A protocol for a systematic review. *BMJ Open*, *13*(3), e068119. https://doi.org/10.1136/bmjopen-2022-068119

Zhou, T., Bao, Y., Guo, D., Bai, Y., Wang, R., Cao, X., Li, H., & Hua, Y. (2022). Intolerance of uncertainty and future career anxiety among Chinese undergraduate students during COVID-19 period: Fear of COVID-19 and depression as mediators. *Frontiers in Public Health*, *10*, 1015446. https://doi.org/10.3389/fpubh.2022.1015446

Zhou, X., Bambling, M., Bai, X., Smith, A. C., & Edirippulige, S. (2023b). Exploring factors affecting Chinese adolescents' perceived usefulness and engagement with a stress management app: A qualitative study. *Frontiers in Psychology*, *14*, 1249093. https://doi.org/10.3389/fpsyg.2023.1249093

Zhu, S., Wang, L., & Gan, Y. (2025). Lying flat to play on smartphone excessively: The role of self-esteem. *Frontiers in Psychology*, *16*, 1516869. https://doi.org/10.3389/fpsyg.2025.1516869

Chapter 2

Stigma and barriers to mental health support among Chinese youth

Olive K. L. Woo

INTRODUCTION

The preceding chapter discussed the silent crisis of mental health challenges among young adults in China, highlighting the pervasive influences of cultural stigmas, academic and career pressures, economic uncertainty, and social media influence. Building on this foundation, this chapter explores the specific barriers that prevent young adults in China from seeking psychological help. Despite growing awareness, stigma and systemic obstacles continue to hinder access to mental healthcare, perpetuating a cycle of silence and emotional suffering. The chapter examines the culture-specific stigma, social and familial pressures, gender-specific stigma, and inadequate psychoeducation in the context of China.

CULTURE-SPECIFIC STIGMA

Under the influence of traditional culture, mental health issues are often considered a sign of weakness in China. It may relate to Confucianism that values social order, harmony, and role fulfilment (Kirmayer & Young, 1998). Studies have shown that Confucianism emphasise self-cultivation, duty, and maintaining social roles, which can stigmatise mental health problems as failures to uphold these obligations (Chen, 2023). This cultural framework fosters a reluctance to acknowledge or seek help for mental illness, as it is often perceived as a threat to family honour and social harmony (Wu et al., 2023). As such, depression and anxiety are often stigmatised and perceived as weaknesses in personality and sources

 DOI: 10.1201/9781003649137-3

of bad thoughts (Kung, 2004; Li et al., 2018; Sun et al., 2018). As a result, practicing self-control and independently solving problems are culturally prioritised over seeking help for mental health issues (Boey, 1999; Loo et al., 1989; Zhang et al., 1998).

Mental health problems are also seen as indicators of disrupted relationships in society (Kolstad & Gjesvik, 2013). The concept "face," or "*lian*," refers to one's and one's family's dignity (Earley, 1997). Preserving interpersonal harmony, or "saving" face, is then crucial (Chen et al., 2005). Such strong emphasis on the family and mental illness can bring shame to the family, leading to the "loss" of face and affecting familial relationships and support systems (Yin et al., 2020). On the broader level, revealing mental illness leads to losing face and brings shame to the social network, the person with mental illness might be shunned, banned, or discriminated within the social network (Yang et al., 2007). The fear of losing face is believed to be a mediating process for stigma in Chinese society (Kleinman & Kleinman, 1993).

Furthermore, misconceptions about mental health have perpetuated its stigma in Chinese societies. Psychotic disorders and mania, for example, are commonly stigmatised due to the perception that these mental health issues would lead to violent behaviours, antisocial activities, and unpredictable actions (Wang et al., 2013; Xu et al., 2018). A cross-sectional study with 1,775 Chinese reveals the high prevalence of mental health stigma, with many Chinese holding negative attitudes towards individuals with mental disorders (Yin et al., 2020). Most Chinese adults and youth have some general knowledge of mental health, but little knowledge about the causes, treatment, and prevention of mental illness (Guo et al., 2020; Yin et al., 2020). Public stigma is especially manifested in discrimination in closer personal realms, holding negative attitudes about having a closer personal relationship with individuals with mental health difficulties (Hao et al., 2023).

SOCIAL AND FAMILIAL PRESSURE

Familial and social attitudes towards mental health have been heavily influenced by the collectivistic ideas that are ingrained in Chinese society. In line with collectivist values, decisions are encouraged to be made collectively as a family or community, rather than individually (Hsiao et al., 2006; Hwang, 2000). Such collectivism is found to be linked with higher levels of mental illness stigma and negative perceptions of mental illness (Papadopoulos et al., 2013). In particular, stigma experienced by the family members of people with mental illness is prominent in Chinese communities due to the deeply rooted concept of "face" and concerns over tainted lineage (Yang et al., 2014 Yin et al., 2020). Family members may experience blaming, being mocked or ridiculed by others (Tawiah et al., 2015).

Even worse, stigmatising terms such as "violent," "crazy," "incapable," and "unfit" are used (Chan et al., 2017; Yu et al., 2018). Coupled with the tendency to avoid close personal relationships with individuals experiencing mental illness (Haraguchi et al., 2009; Yin et al., 2020), those affected often face familial and social pressure and feel compelled to hide their conditions due to fear of hostility (Mak et al., 2014; Yu et al., 2018). Such concealment would lead to delays in treatment and rehabilitation, and to maladaptive coping strategies to avoid the stigma.

Furthermore, emotional expressions are often discouraged in Chinese society. Emotional self-control, restraint, and suppression are contrarily valued for maintaining interpersonal harmony, a principle deeply rooted in Confucian values that emphasise social cohesion and collective well-being (Markus & Kitayama, 1991; Wang et al., 2023). Extreme emotional reactions are typically avoided and discouraged because they are perceived as threats to interpersonal relationships and group cohesion (Lin et al., 1995; Zhang et al., 2024). Research shows that while chronic emotional suppression can lead to increased stress and adverse physical health outcomes, the cultural context in China moderates these effects, often framing emotional control as beneficial for psychosomatic health (Chen et al., 2005). Such emotional suppression is closely intertwined with the concept of "face", which serves as a strategy to protect both personal and familial dignity in the Chinese context (Wu & Chen, 2023; Yang & Kleinman, 2008).

GENDER-SPECIFIC STIGMA

Gender expectations for men to be stoic and women to be self-sacrificing has perpetuated stigma in China. Chinese society is a patriarchal society, where masculinity is highly endorsed (Levant et al., 1996). Chinese men place particular importance on upholding cultural expectations to be the protector of the family (Hibbins, 2005; Lin, 2013). Under this cultural ideal, Chinese men are expected to be strong and able to endure pain without showing feelings. Sayings such as "a man should not easily shed his tears" (「男兒有淚不輕彈」) and "Real men would rather bleed than weep" (「大丈夫流血不流淚」) suggest that men should endure pain and hardship without showing emotions (Yeung et al., 2015). The conformation of masculine norms and controlling emotional expressions has been found to be associated with a lower tendency to seek psychological help (Burns & Mahalik, 2006; Xin, 2024).

On the other hand, Chinese women are culturally expected to be self-sacrificing for the common good. Chinese women tend to internalise the gender role of being self-sacrificing, believing that being a good woman equates to being "sensitive to the needs of others" and "not allowed to ask for my own needs to be met" (Tang & Tang, 2001). Women with a higher tendency for self-sacrifice are more prone to feeling guilty if they focus more on self-care, which negatively impacts their recovery of mental health conditions (Maji & Dixit, 2019). The perceived gender role of being subjugated also discourages Chinese women from seeking help from both formal and informal sources for their mental health issues (Chiu, 2004).

INADEQUATE PSYCHOEDUCATION AND AWARENESS

Enhancing public awareness of mental health issues and promoting understanding of mental illness can normalise help-seeking behaviours (Chen, 2018; Yu et al., 2018). Public education campaigns that improve mental health literacy, such as psychoeducational sessions on topics including awareness and causes of mental health can reduce stigma and encourage individuals to seek help when needed (Yang et al., 2023). However, systemic mental health education appears to be inadequate in China (Zhang & Du, 2018). In schools, teachers are responsible for providing mental health education in addition to their academic duties (Yao et al., 2021). However, a large portion of primary and secondary school teachers in China lack adequate professional training and resources for mental health education (Yao et al., 2021). In the workplace, mental health education appears to be underdeveloped as well. Only recently there has been some attention placed on mental health support, with the emergence of digital mental health interventions and support platforms (Sun et al., 2013, 2022).

CONCLUSIONS

This chapter has explored the multifaceted barriers that young adults in China face when seeking mental health support. Despite growing awareness, these obstacles continue to perpetuate a culture of silence, preventing many from accessing the care they need. However, the advancement in technology appears to be an option to break these barriers by providing anonymous, accessible platforms. The next chapter will explore how AI can serve as an innovative mental health companion, assisting young people to navigate their mental health challenges with less barriers.

REFERENCES

Boey, K. W. (1999). Help-seeking preference of college students in urban China after the implementation of the "open-door" policy. *International Journal of Social Psychiatry*, *45*(2), 104–116.

Burns, S. M., & Mahalik, J. R. (2006). Physical health, self-reliance, and emotional control as moderators of relationship between locus of control and mental health among men treated for. *Journal of Behavioral Medicine*, *29*, 561–572.

Chan, S. K., Ching, E. Y., Lam, K. S., So, H. C., Hui, C. L., Lee, E. H., … & Chen, E. Y. (2017). Newspaper coverage of mental illness in Hong Kong between 2002 and 2012: Impact of introduction of a new Chinese name of psychosis. *Early Intervention in Psychiatry*, *11*(4), 342–345.

Chen, J. (2018). Some people may need it, but not me, not now: Seeking professional help for mental health problems in urban China. *Transcultural Psychiatry*, *55*(6), 754–774.

Chen, S.-W. (2023). Learning motivations and effort beliefs in Confucian cultural context: A dual-mode theoretical framework of achievement goal. *Frontiers in Psychology*, *14*, 1058456–1058456. https://doi.org/10.3389/fpsyg.2023.1058456

Chen, S. X., Cheung, F. M., Bond, M. H., & Leung, J. P. (2005). Decomposing the construct of ambivalence over emotional expression in a Chinese cultural context. *European Journal of Personality*, *19*(3), 185–204.

Chiu, M. Y.-L. (2004). Why Chinese women do not seek help: A cultural perspective on the psychology of women. *Counselling Psychology Quarterly*, *17*(2), 155–166.

Earley, P. C. (1997). *Face, Harmony, and Social Structure: An Analysis of Organizational Behavior Across Cultures*. Oxford University Press.

Guo, S., Yang, Y., Liu, F., & Li, F. (2020). The awareness rate of mental health knowledge Among Chinese adolescent: A systematic review and meta-analysis. *Medicine*, *99*(7), e19148. https://doi.org/10.1097/MD.0000000000019148

Hao, Y., Wu, Q., Wang, X., Ma, Y., Wang, Y., Peng, P., Wang, X., Yang, Q., Liu, Y., Li, M., He, L., Wang, Q., Zhou, Y., Liu, T., & Chen, S. (2023). Stigmatizing attitudes toward mental illness among caregivers of patients with mental disorders in China. *Frontiers in Public Health*, *11*, 1071954–1071954. https://doi.org/10.3389/fpubh.2023.1071954

Haraguchi, K., Maeda, M., Mei, Y. X., & Uchimura, N. (2009). Stigma associated with schizophrenia: Cultural comparison of social distance in Japan and China. *Psychiatry and Clinical Neurosciences*, *63*(2), 153–160.

Hibbins, R. (2005). Migration and gender identity among Chinese skilled migrants in Australia. *Geoforum*, *36*, 167–180.

Hsiao, F. H., Klimidis, S., Minas, H., & Tan, E. S. (2006). Cultural attribution of mental health suffering in Chinese societies: The views of Chinese patients with mental illness and their caregivers. *Journal of Clinical Nursing*, *15*(8), 998–1006.

Hwang, K. K. (2000). Chinese relationalism: Theoretical construction and methodological considerations. *Journal for the Theory of Social Behaviour*, *30*(2), 155–178.

Kirmayer, L. J., & Young, A. (1998). Culture and somatization: Clinical, epidemiological, and ethnographic perspectives. *Psychosomatic Medicine*, *60*(4), 420–430.

Kleinman, A., & Kleinman, J. (1993). Face, favor and families: The social course of mental health problems in Chinese and American societies. *Chinese Journal of Mental Health*, *6*, 37–47.

Kolstad, A., & Gjesvik, N. (2013). The importance of harmonious relationships for mental health in traditional Chinese society. *International Journal of Culture and Mental Health*, *6*(3), 193–207.

Kung, W. W. (2004). Cultural and practical barriers to seeking mental health treatment for Chinese Americans. *Journal of Community Psychology*, *32*(1), 27–43.

Levant, R. F., Wu, R., & Fischer, J. (1996). Masculinity ideology: A comparison between US and Chinese young men and women. *Journal of Gender, Culture, and Health*, *1*, 207–220.

Li, A., Jiao, D., & Zhu, T. (2018). Detecting depression stigma on social media: A linguistic analysis. *Journal of Affective Disorders*, *232*, 358–362.

Lin, T. Y., Tseng, W. S., & Ye, Y. (1995). *Chinese Societies and Mental Health*. Oxford University Press.

Lin, X. (2013). 'Filial son', the family and identity formation among male migrant workers in urban China. *Gender, Place and Culture*, *21*, 717–732.

Loo, C., Tong, B., & True, R. (1989). A bitter bean: Mental health status and attitudes in Chinatown. *Journal of Community Psychology*, *17*, 283–296.

Maji, S., & Dixit, S. (2019). Rev. of Self-silencing and women's health: A review. *International Journal of Social Psychiatry*, *65*(1), 3–13.

Mak, W. W., Chong, E. S., & Wong, C. C. (2014). Beyond attributions: Understanding public stigma of mental illness with the common sense model. *American Journal of Orthopsychiatry*, *84*, 173–181.

Markus, H. R., & Kitayama, S. (1991). Culture and the self: Implications for cognition, emotion, and motivation. *Psychological Review*, *98*, 224–253.

Papadopoulos, C., Foster, J., & Caldwell, K. (2013). 'Individualism-collectivism' as an explanatory device for mental illness stigma. *Community Mental Health Journal*, *49*(3), 270–280.

Sun, J., Buys, N., & Wang, X. (2013). Effectiveness of a workplace-based intervention program to promote mental health among employees in privately owned enterprises in China. *Population Health Management*, *16*(6), 406–414.

Sun, K. S., Lam, T. P., & Wu, D. (2018). Chinese perspectives on primary care for common mental disorders: Barriers and policy implications. *International Journal of Social Psychiatry*, *64*(5), 417–426.

Sun, S., Zhang, Z., Tian, M., Mougenot, C., Glozier, N., & Calvo, R. A. (2022). Preferences for a mental health support technology among Chinese employees: Mixed methods approach. *JMIR Human Factors*, *9*(4), e40933.

Tang, T. N., & Tang, C. S. (2001). Gender role internalization, multiple roles, and Chinese women's mental health. *Psychology of Women Quarterly*, *25*(3), 181–196.

Tawiah, P. E., Adongo, P. B., & Aikins, M. (2015). Mental health-related stigma and discrimination in Ghana: Experience of patients and their caregivers. *Ghana Medical Journal*, *49*(1), 30–36.

Wang, J. Y., He, L. Y., Jiang, Q., Cai, J., Wang, W. L., et al. (2013). Mental health literacy among residents in Shanghai. *Shanghai Archives of Psychiatry*, *25*(4), 224–235.

Wang, P. S., Berglund, P., Olfson, M., Pincus, H. A., Wells, K. B., & Kessler, R. C. (2005). Failure and delay in initial treatment contact after first onset of mental disorders in the National Comorbidity Survey Replication. *Archives of General Psychiatry*, *62*(6), 603–613.

Wang, Y., Lau, J. T. F., & Chan, K. L. (2023). Unraveling Chinese talk about emotion: The interplay of culture, language, and somatization. *Frontiers in Psychology*. https://www.frontiersin.org/journals/psychology/articles/10.3389/fpsyg.2023.1157863/full

Wu, Y., & Chen, L. (2023). Cultural norms and emotional regulation: A qualitative study among Chinese and Taiwanese adults. *Journal of Cross-Cultural Psychology*, *54*(1), 89–105.

Wu, Y., Chiu, M. Y. L., Wu, W., Han, S., & Wang, J. (2023). What makes Chinese adolescents "trapped" in severe mental illness? An interactionist perspective on self and identity. *International Journal of Qualitative Studies on Health and Well-Being*, *18*(1), 2250093–2250093. https://doi.org/10.1080/17482631.2023.2250093

Xin, H. (2024). Gender Stereotypes and Health of Individuals in China: The Role of Education and Gender. *Journal of Student Research*, *13*(1).

Xu, X., Li, X.-M., Zhang, J., & Wang, W. (2018). Mental health-related stigma in China. *Issues in Mental Health Nursing*, *39*(2), 126–134.

Yang, J., Li, Y., Gao, R., Chen, H., & Yang, Z. (2023). Relationship between mental health literacy and professional psychological help-seeking attitudes in China: A chain mediation model. *BMC Psychiatry*, *23*(1), 956.

Yang, L. H., & Kleinman, A. (2008). 'Face' and the embodiment of stigma in China: the cases of schizophrenia and AIDS. *Social science & medicine (1982)*, *67*(3), 398–408. https://doi.org/10.1016/j.socscimed.2008.03.011

Yang, L. H., Kleinman, A., Link, B. G., Phelan, J. C., Lee, S., & Good, B. (2007). Culture and stigma: Adding moral experience to stigma theory. *Social Science & Medicine (1982)*, *64*(7), 1524–1535. https://doi.org/10.1016/j.socscimed.2006.11.013

Yang, L. H., Lai, G. Y., Tu, M., Luo, M., Wonpat-Borja, A., Jackson, V. W., ... & Dixon, L. (2014). A brief anti-stigma intervention for Chinese immigrant caregivers of individuals with psychosis: Adaptation and initial findings. *Transcultural Psychiatry*, *51*(2), 139–157.

Yao, M., Kadetz, P. I., Sidibe, A. M., Wu, Y., Li, J., Lyu, J., ... & Hesketh, T. (2021). Teachers' perceptions of student mental health in eastern China: A qualitative study. *International Journal of Environmental Research and Public Health*, *18*(14), 7271.

Yeung, N. C., Mak, W. W., & Cheung, L. K. (2015). Conformity to the emotional-control masculine norm and psychological well-being among Chinese men in Hong Kong: The mediating role of stress appraisal for expressing tender emotions. *Psychology of Men & Masculinity*, *16*(3), 304.

Yin, H., Wardenaar, K. J., Xu, G., Tian, H., & Schoevers, R. A. (2020). Mental health stigma and mental health knowledge in Chinese population: A cross-sectional study. *BMC Psychiatry*, *20*(1), 323. https://doi.org/10.1186/s12888-020-02705-x

Yu, S., Kowitt, S. D., Fisher, E. B., & Li, G. (2018). Mental health in China: Stigma, family obligations, and the potential of peer support. *Community Mental Health Journal*, *54*, 757–764.

Zhang, A. Y., Snowden, L. R., & Sue, S. (1998). Differences between Asian and White Americans' help seeking and utilization patterns in the Los Angeles area. *Journal of Community Psychology*, *26*(4), 317–326.

Zhang, H., & Du, Y. (2018). Chinese school curricula should include mental health education. *The Lancet Psychiatry*, *5*(8), e18.

Zhang, H., Li, X., & Wang, Y. (2024). Childhood trauma, emotion regulation, peer attachment, and family dynamics in Chinese populations. *Unpublished manuscript*. https://www.carterfunkhouser.com/publication/zhang-2024/Zhang2024.pdf

Chapter 3

Artificial intelligence as mental health companion

Olive K. L. Woo

INTRODUCTION

The mental health crisis among young people in China has exposed significant gaps in the availability and accessibility of traditional mental health services. From the rising prevalence of anxiety and depression to the pervasive stigma surrounding mental health, many individuals are left without the essential support they need, as discussed in the previous chapters. In response to these challenges, artificial intelligence (AI) has emerged as an innovative and possible solution which offers scalable, non-judgemental, and round-the-clock support, potentially filling the void. It appears to not only addressing the resource shortages but also providing a culturally sensitive alternative, particularly for young people hesitant to seek help through conventional means. This chapter discusses the potential role of AI to support mental health, exploring its capabilities and advantages.

AVAILABILITY, ACCESSIBILITY, AND AFFORDABILITY

AI-powered mental health applications are available on a 24/7 basis, providing immediate support whenever needed, which is particularly valuable during crises or outside traditional office hours (Baek et al., 2025; Khawaja & Bélisle-Pipon, 2023). This around-the-clock accessibility enables users to receive real-time guidance and coping strategies, helping to bridge gaps in mental health care, especially for those without regular access to professionals (Thakkar et al., 2024).

DOI: 10.1201/9781003649137-4

Accessible via smartphones, these AI chatbots and apps can reach underserved populations in remote or low-income regions, offering timely mental health support without the need for appointments or transportation. Their continuous, on-demand assistance benefits individuals with demanding schedules or those living in isolated areas (Khawaja & Bélisle-Pipon, 2023). AI systems are highly scalable, capable of supporting large numbers of users simultaneously, enhancing affordability and broadening reach (Baek et al., 2025). Furthermore, AI tools provide low-cost and affordable options that make mental health support attainable for underserved populations or individuals with financial difficulties (Ni & Jia, 2025; Yong et al., 2025). One comprehensive review has shown AI-driven treatments reduce average costs by approximately 33% compared to conventional therapy sessions, while also shortening treatment duration (Yadav, 2021).

Non-judgemental and anonymous nature

One key advantage of AI-driven mental health tools is to provide a non-judgemental and anonymous platform. Elaborated in Chapter 2, some Chinese youth may hesitate to seek traditional mental health support due to fear of stigma or judgement, especially in cultures where mental health remains taboo. AI chatbots mitigate these barriers by offering a private space where users can express concerns freely without labelling or stigmatisation (Chaudhry and Debi, 2024; Lancet, 2022). Studies have shown that some users feel more comfortable disclosing sensitive issues to AI-assisted tools than to human providers, which can encourage earlier intervention and support (Chaudhry and Debi, 2024).

Personalised support

AI systems excel at personalising mental health support by adapting responses to individual user input. Machine learning algorithms can learn from user interactions, preferences, and behavioural patterns to offer tailored advice, coping strategies, and resources (Baek et al., 2025). For instance, AI-driven chatbots can provide tailored, psychological support, such as *Youper* as a chatbot for personalised mental health assessment, instant support via conversations, and symptom monitoring; *Wysa* for managing anxiety, depression, and chronic pain (Leo et al., 2022; Mehta et al., 2021;

Sinha et al., 2023); and *Gabby* for lifestyle modification and stress management (Gardiner et al., 2017).

Empathetic simulation

AI is able to simulate empathetic interactions in mental health tools through advanced techniques such as natural language processing and sentiment analysis. These technologies enable chatbots to detect subtle emotional cues in user text or speech, allowing them to tailor responses that align with the user's emotional state and needs (Denecke & Gabarron, 2024; Malgaroli et al., 2023). The large language models, such as ChatGPT and DeepSeek-V3, have trained on large amount of unlabelled text that improves computers' ability to process words (Brown et al., 2020; Zhou et al., 2024). A pilot study by Melo et al. (2023) indicates that ChatGPT could serve as an engaging and useful tool for delivering evidence-based mental health support to individuals in psychiatric wards.

Linguistic and cultural adaptation

AI tools can be developed to resonate with the linguistic, cultural, and emotional intricacies of particular populations. DeepSeek (see Part II), for example, provides support that tailored to Chinese language and values, enabling more authentic and effective communication. It also provides anonymous, non-judgemental support that aligns with cultural expectations such as family dynamics and the concept of "saving face." This encourages individuals to seek help without fear of social repercussions, a barrier especially significant in societies like China where reputation and family honour heavily influence mental health care seeking (Day, 2023). Users have reported in news that DeepSeek offers empathetic and culturally aligned responses that provide counselling and psychological support (BBC News, 2024; NDTV, 2025). Research has also shown that culturally adapted digital interventions can ensure accessibility and the sustained use of digital health interventions (Naderbagi et al., 2024).

CONCLUSIONS

This chapter highlights the potential of AI in mental health care, focusing on its key capabilities: availability, anonymity, empathetic simulation, personalised support, and cultural adaptation. These strengths are increasingly validated by peer-reviewed research. However, alongside these advancements, significant challenges persist—such as privacy concerns, algorithmic bias, and the risk of overreliance on AI without adequate human oversight. These issues will be explored further in Chapter 7. As this rapidly evolving field progresses, rigorous research and clinical studies remain essential to refining AI's role in mental health care, a topic to be discussed in Chapter 9. The next section introduces DeepSeek and its unique role in providing mental health support.

REFERENCES

Baek, G., Cha, C., & Han, J.-H. (2025). AI chatbots for psychological health for health professionals: Scoping review. *JMIR Human Factors, 12*, e67682. https://doi.org/10.2196/67682

BBC News. (2024, May 16). *China's AI-powered 'war preparedness' rail network unveiled.* Retrieved from https://www.bbc.com/news/articles/cy7g45g2nxno

Brown, T. B., Mann, B., Ryder, N., Subbiah, M., Kaplan, J., Dhariwal, P., Neelakantan, A., Shyam, P., Sastry, G., Askell, A., Agarwal, S., Herbert-Voss, A., Krueger, G., Henighan, T., Child, R., Ramesh, A., Ziegler, D. M., Wu, J., Winter, C., … Amodei, D. (2020). *Language Models are Few-Shot Learners.* https://doi.org/10.48550/arxiv.2005.14165

Chaudhry, B. M., & Debi, H. R. (2024). User perceptions and experiences of an AI-driven conversational agent for mental health support. *mHealth, 10*, 22. https://doi.org/10.21037/mhealth-23-55

Day, M. J. (2023). Towards ethical artificial intelligence in universities: ChatGPT, culture, and mental health stigmas in Asian higher education post COVID-19. *Journal of Technology in Counselor Education and Supervision, 4*(1). https://doi.org/10.61888/2692-4129.1097

Denecke, K., & Gabarron, E. (2024). The ethical aspects of integrating sentiment and emotion analysis in chatbots for depression intervention. *Frontiers in Psychiatry, 15*, 1462083. https://doi.org/10.3389/fpsyt.2024.1462083

Gardiner, P. M., McCue, K. D., Negash, L. M., Cheng, T., White, L. F., Yinusa-Nyahkoon, L., Jack, B. W., & Bickmore, T. W. (2017). Engaging women with an embodied conversational agent to deliver mindfulness and lifestyle recommendations: A feasibility randomized control trial. *Patient Education and Counseling, 100*(9), 1720–1729. https://doi.org/10.1016/j.pec.2017.04.015

Khawaja, Z., & Bélisle-Pipon, J.-C. (2023). Your robot therapist is not your therapist: Understanding the role of AI-powered mental health chatbots. *Frontiers in Digital Health*, *5*, 1278186–1278186. https://doi.org/10.3389/fdgth.2023.1278186

Leo, A. J., Schuelke, M. J., Hunt, D. M., Metzler, J. P., Miller, J. P., Areán, P. A., Armbrecht, M. A., & Cheng, A. L. (2022). A digital mental health intervention in an orthopedic setting for patients with symptoms of depression and/or anxiety: Feasibility prospective cohort study. *JMIR Formative Research*, *6*(2):e34889. https://doi.org/10.2196/34889

Malgaroli, M., Hull, T. D., Zech, J. M. et al. (2023) Natural language processing for mental health interventions: A systematic review and research framework. *Translational Psychiatry*, *13*, 309. https://doi.org/10.1038/s41398-023-02592-2

Mehta, A., Niles, A. N., Vargas, J. H., Marafon, T., Couto, D. D., & Gross, J. J. (2021). Acceptability and effectiveness of artificial intelligence therapy for anxiety and depression (youper): Longitudinal observational study. *Journal of Medical Internet Research*, *23*(6), e26771. https://doi.org/10.2196/26771

Melo, A., Simões, F., Silva, C., Santos, V., Silva, I., Lopes, J., & Carnot, M. J. (2023). ChatGPT: A promising tool for mental health support in psychiatric inpatient care. *Neuroscience Applied*, *2*, 102558. https://doi.org/10.1016/j.nsa.2023.102558

Naderbagi, A., Loblay, V., Zahed, I. U. M., Ekambareshwar, M., Poulsen, A., Song, Y. J. C., Ospina-Pinillos, L., Krausz, M., Mamdouh Kamel, M., Hickie, I. B., & LaMonica, H. M. (2024). Cultural and contextual adaptation of digital health interventions: Narrative review. *Journal of Medical Internet Research*, *26*, e55130. https://doi.org/10.2196/55130

NDTV (2025 Feb 13). *Why young people in China are turning to AI for emotional support*. Retrieved from https://www.ndtv.com/india-news/why-young-people-in-china-are-turning-to-ai-for-emotional-support-7699175

Ni, Y., & Jia, F. (2025). A scoping review of AI-driven digital interventions in mental health care: Mapping applications across screening, support, monitoring, prevention, and clinical education. *Healthcare*, *13*(10), 1205. https://doi.org/10.3390/healthcare13101205

Sinha, C., Meheli, S., & Kadaba, M. (2023). Understanding digital mental health needs and usage with an artificial intelligence-led mental health app (Wysa) during the COVID-19 pandemic: Retrospective analysis. *JMIR Formative Research*, *26*(7), e41913. https://doi.org/10.2196/41913

Thakkar, A., Gupta, A., & De Sousa, A. (2024). Artificial intelligence in positive mental health: A narrative review. *Frontiers in Digital Health*, *6*, 1280235. https://doi.org/10.3389/fdgth.2024.1280235

The Lancet. (2022). Mental health after China's prolonged lockdowns. *The Lancet (British Edition)*, *399*(10342), 2167–2167. https://doi.org/10.1016/S0140-6736(22)01051-0

Yadav, V. (2021). AI and economics of mental health: Analyzing how AI can be used to improve the cost-effectiveness of mental health treatments and interventions. *Journal of Scientific and Engineering Research*, *8*(7), 274–284.

Yong, E., Teo, Y. N., & Yong, K. H. (2025). AI technology: A new game changer for the future mental health industry? *Asia-Pacific Journal of Public Health*, *37*(1), 148–149. https://doi.org/10.1177/10105395241303790

Zhou, H., Liu, F., Gu, B., Zou, X., Huang, J., Wu, J., Li, Y., Chen, S. S., Zhou, P., Liu, J., Hua, Y., Mao, C., You, C., Wu, X., Zheng, Y., Clifton, L., Li, Z., Luo, J., & Clifton, D. A. (2024). A survey of large language models in medicine: Progress, application, and challenge. https://doi.org/10.48550/arxiv.2311.05112

Part II

DeepSeek and the rise of AI for emotional support

Chapter 4

Foundations of DeepSeek: How it works

M. W. Geda and Yuk Ming Tang

INTRODUCTION: ORIGINS AND DESIGN PHILOSOPHY OF DEEPSEEK

DeepSeek AI emerged as a start-up in China around mid-2023, with a vision to advance AI through accessible and efficient technologies (Singh et al., 2025). The company emphasises open-source principles to foster widespread innovation and collaboration in the field (Deng et al., 2025). At its core, the design approach prioritises resource optimisation, enabling high-performance models with reduced computational demands and lower development costs compared to industry giants. The model, developed for just $5.58 million, a fraction of the cost of its Western counterparts, achieved remarkable efficiency (Sallam et al., 2025). This philosophy stems from a need to democratise advanced AI, making it viable for diverse applications without excessive resource barriers. Early influences include building on scalable architectures to address real-world challenges such as reasoning and efficiency, positioning DeepSeek as a disruptor in global AI landscapes (Deng et al., 2025).

DeepSeek prioritises advanced reasoning capabilities as its foundational pillar, distinguishing it from general purpose large language models (LLMs). Unlike architectures optimised primarily for pattern recognition or text generation, DeepSeek embeds logical inference, causal analysis, and multi-step problem-solving directly into its core design (Xiang et al., 2025). This approach enables the model to excel in complex domains such as math, clinical diagnosis, and algorithmic design, where structured reasoning is paramount (Deng et al., 2025). To balance performance with computational efficiency, DeepSeek leverages a Mixture-of-Experts (MoE) architecture (Dai et al., 2024; DeepSeek-AI, Zhu, et al., 2024).

DOI: 10.1201/9781003649137-6

MoE enables task-specific scaling: DeepSeek-Coder uses coding-focused experts, while DeepSeek-Math employs mathematically tuned pathways (DeepSeek-AI, Zhu, et al., 2024; Shao et al., 2024). This design dynamically routes each input token to specialised sub-networks ("experts"), activating only relevant pathways during inference (Dai et al., 2024).

DeepSeek's foundational choices, reasoning-centric design to MoE efficiency, enable unprecedented cost-to-performance ratios. DeepSeek-R1 operates at 1/20th–1/50th the cost of comparable models such as OpenAI's o1 while matching or exceeding their capabilities in specialised domains (Baptista, 2025). More than mere engineering trade-offs, these principles represent a paradigm shift: proving that specialised, transparent, and accessible AI can outperform generalised models in efficiency and effectiveness (Deng et al., 2025). This democratising vision positions DeepSeek as both a technical disruptor and a catalyst for equitable AI adoption worldwide.

This chapter explores the foundational elements of DeepSeek through various critical perspectives. First, the chapter discusses DeepSeek's Evolution Timeline to trace the model's development from its 2023 inception to the current V3.1, highlighting key milestones and iterative advancements. Next, it examines the DeepSeek-R1 Architectural Foundation to analyse its Mixture of Experts (MoE) implementation, transformer innovations, and scaling laws that drive efficiency and performance. The chapter then investigates the Model Training Pipeline. It also explores the Thought Process, focusing on chain-of-reasoning transparency and self-verification mechanisms that enhance output reliability and interpretability. The chapter further discusses Empathetic Responsiveness to highlight emotion-aware output tuning, emphasising DeepSeek's human-centric approach. Additionally, it covers Cross-Cultural Capabilities to evaluate its multilingual design and cultural-context adaptation for global applicability. Finally, the chapter reviews Comparative Benchmarks to assess DeepSeek's performance against leading models such as GPT-4o and Claude 3.5.

DEEPSEEK EVOLUTION TIMELINE

DeepSeek's technical journey began in November 2023 with two foundational releases: the code-specialised DeepSeek Coder

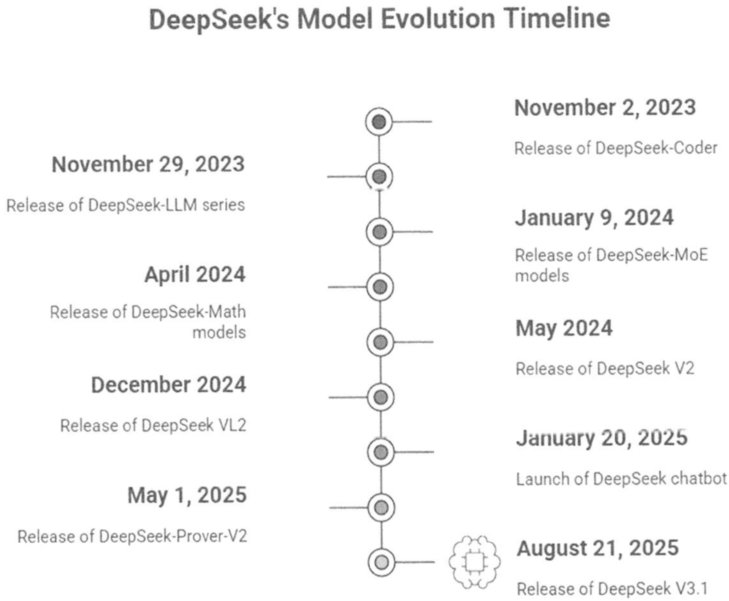

Figure 4.1 DeepSeek's journey: Key milestones and innovations.

(DeepSeek-AI, Zhu, et al., 2024) followed by the general-purpose DeepSeek-LLM series (DeepSeek-AI, Bi, et al., 2024). Figure 4.1 visually summarises the rapid evolution of DeepSeek, highlighting ten major milestones achieved in less than two years.

These releases underpinned DeepSeek's commitment to advancing both specialised and general AI capabilities in parallel, a strategy that would continue to define its roadmap (Zhao et al., 2025). From the outset, DeepSeek adopted an aggressive release, iterating and expanding its technology stack at a remarkable pace. Each release has built upon the last, demonstrating a clear trajectory of increasing sophistication, capability, and utility.

DEEPSEEK-R1 ARCHITECTURAL FOUNDATION

DeepSeek-R1 is a significant advancement introduced by DeepSeek in January 2025 under the MIT License. Building upon the established DeepSeek-V3-Base architecture, the DeepSeek-R1 model incorporates MoE approach, leveraging transformer innovations to enhance logical inference, mathematical reasoning, and real-time problem-solving capabilities (Deepseek-Ai/DeepSeek-R1 · Hugging Face, 2025; Mercer et al., 2025).

A defining feature of DeepSeek-R1 is its highly modular, transformer-decoder-based architecture, consisting of a total of 61 layers. The initial three layers are implemented as dense transformers, responsible for capturing generalisable features and providing a strong foundational representation for subsequent processing. The remaining 58 layers are composed of specialised Mixture-of-Experts (MoE) blocks, each containing multiple expert networks that are selectively activated based on the input context (see Figure 4.2) (Dahlke et al., 2025). This hybrid design balances depth and efficiency, enabling state-of-the-art reasoning while minimising computational overhead. This hybrid design achieves an effective balance between model depth and computational efficiency, allowing

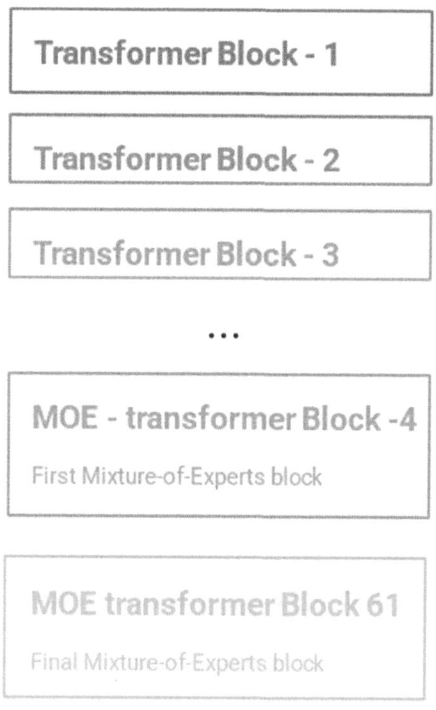

Figure 4.2 Illustration of the DeepSeek-R1 architectural foundation.

DeepSeek-R1 to deliver state-of-the-art reasoning capabilities while maintaining manageable computational overhead (Li et al., 2025).

In addition to its architectural sophistication, DeepSeek-R1 supports rich multimodal functionalities, seamlessly processing images, code, and text within a unified framework (Puspitasari et al., 2025). This enables a broad range of applications, from complex mathematical problem-solving to advanced code generation and image understanding. The model's versatility and efficiency make it particularly well-suited for real-world deployments requiring high accuracy, adaptability, and transparency.

DEEPSEEK-R1 MODEL TRAINING

The training of DeepSeek-R1 involves a multi-stage pipeline of supervised fine-tuning (SFT) and reinforcement learning (RL) to achieve state-of-the-art performance, particularly in mathematical and coding reasoning. The multi-stage pipeline (Figure 4.3) is an intentional design choice that balances the development of raw reasoning ability with the refinement of human-aligned outputs, leading to a more stable and high-performing model.

The training process includes the following steps:

- Stage 1: "Cold start" Phase. During this stage the base model is fine-tuned on a small, high-quality dataset of "Chain-of-Thought" (CoT) reasoning examples. This provides a strong initial foundation for logical reasoning and structured output, which helps the subsequent RL training to converge more effectively and quickly (DeepSeek-AI, Guo, et al., 2025).
- Stage 2: Reasoning-Oriented Reinforcement Learning (RL). The model's reasoning capabilities are optimised on structured tasks such as math, coding, and logic using a rule-based reward system (DeepSeek-AI, Guo, et al., 2025). This stage is similar to the pure RL approach used for the earlier DeepSeek-R1-Zero model (Deepseek-Ai/DeepSeek-R1-Zero · Hugging Face, 2025), but with added features such as a "language consistency reward" (Park et al., 2025) to mitigate issues of language mixing.
- Stage 3: This stage involves supervised fine-tuning (Dong et al., 2024) on RL Outputs. High-quality reasoning examples generated by the model in Stage 2 are combined with data from

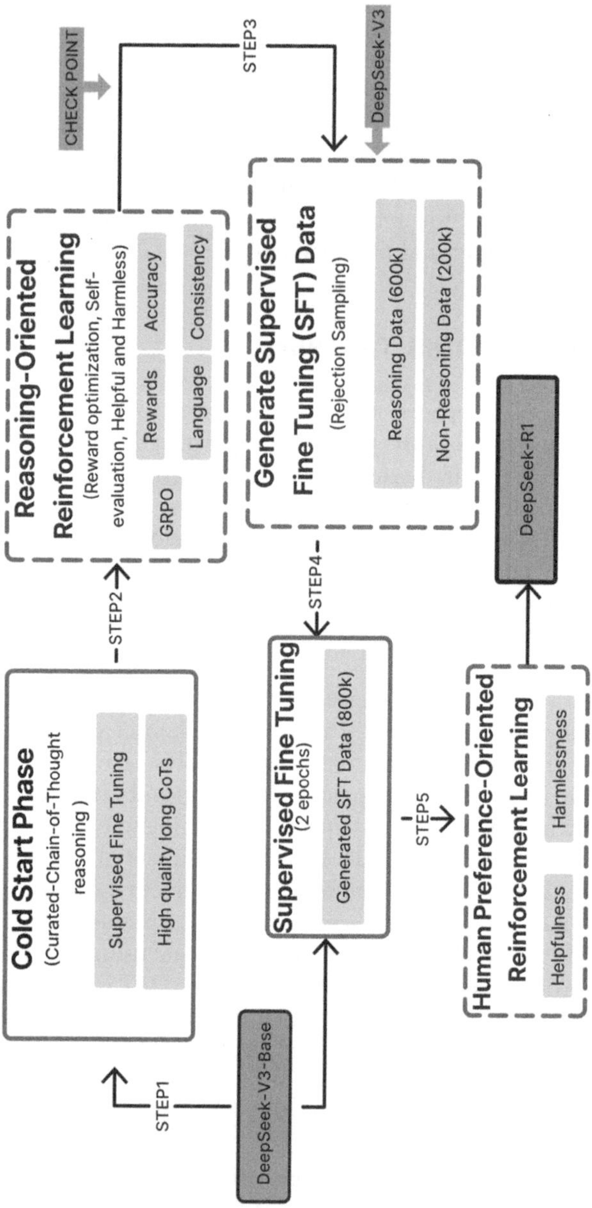

Figure 4.3 DeepSeek-R1's multi-stage training pipeline.

other domains (e.g. writing and Q&A). This new, filtered dataset is used for another round of supervised fine-tuning to further solidify reasoning skills and maintain broader capabilities (DeepSeek-AI, Guo, et al., 2025).

- Stage 4: General Reinforcement Learning. In the final stage, the model is refined to align with human preferences for helpfulness, harmlessness, and overall naturalness. This stage uses human-preference-based RL (Peng et al., 2025), leveraging aspects of the DeepSeek-V3 pipeline (DeepSeek-AI, Liu, et al., 2025).

This training approach results in a more stable, adaptable, and high-performing model, optimised not only for complex mathematical and coding tasks but also for broader reasoning and language understanding across varied contexts.

DEEPSEEK'S "THOUGHT PROCESS": TRANSPARENT AI REASONING

DeepSeek redefines transparency in AI problem-solving by employing explicit CoT decomposition, reinforced by Group Relative Policy Optimisation (GRPO) (Deng et al., 2025). As illustrated in Figure 4.4 (math solving example), DeepSeek's reasoning unfolds step by step in a structured, auditable format. Each mathematical manipulation, such as isolating a square root, squaring both sides, and rearranging terms, is clearly documented. DeepSeek flags pivotal moments, pausing to check for mathematical validity (e.g., assessing whether the discriminant is positive before reporting solutions). This approach not only mimics how expert humans self-monitor but also makes every inference traceable and open to review. By combining CoT with GRPO, DeepSeek ensures that its logical steps are not only transparent but also robust and consistent across similar problems.

EMPATHY AND EMOTIONAL RESPONSIVENESS IN MODEL OUTPUTS

DeepSeek-R1 integrate mechanisms for sentiment detection and aims to generate responses that acknowledge user feelings and offer

Question: Solve for all real x such that $\sqrt{x+2}+\sqrt{5-x}=5$.

Response: <think >

To solve the equation $\sqrt{x+2}+\sqrt{5-x}=5$, let's proceed step by step:

First, isolate one of the square roots:

$\sqrt{x+2}=5-\sqrt{5-x}$

Now, square both sides:

$(\sqrt{x+2})^2=(5-\sqrt{5-x})^2$
$\Rightarrow x+2=25-10\sqrt{5-x}+(5-x)$

Combine like terms:
$x+2=30-x-10\sqrt{5-x}$

Bring terms involving x to one side:
$2x-28=-10\sqrt{5-x}$

Divide both sides by -10:
$\frac{28-2x}{10}=\sqrt{5-x}$
Now, square both sides again:
$\left(\frac{28-2x}{10}\right)^2=5-x$
$\Rightarrow \frac{(28-2x)^2}{100}=5-x$
Multiply both sides by 100:
$(28-2x)^2=100(5-x)$

Expand:
$784-112x+4x^2=500-100x$

Bring all terms to one side:
$4x^2-12x+284=0$

Wait, let's pause. Here's an important check: is the discriminant positive?

Calculate the discriminant:
$(-12)^2-4\cdot4\cdot284=144-4544=-4400$

Since the discriminant is negative, there are **no real solutions.**

Final Answer: There are no real solutions to the equation.

Figure 4.4 Illustration of DeepSeek's CoT reasoning process for solving a mathematical equation.

supportive guidance (Huang & Wang, 2025). Responses are crafted to mirror emotional states, providing affirmation and practical suggestions while maintaining a warm, non-judgemental tone to encourage openness. This is part of a broader trend in AI development to create more "socially intelligent" and "human-centric" AI systems (Tang et al., 2025). Advanced embeddings help fuse emotional awareness into dialogues, ensuring outputs feel authentic and connected rather than mechanical (Rasool et al., 2025). While not fully replicating human intuition, this feature supports applications in mental health or personal advice, where sensitivity to emotions enhances user engagement.

COMPARATIVE BENCHMARKS

Reasoning and coding excellence

Comparative benchmarks across multiple leading AI models reveal DeepSeek's exceptional performance in both reasoning and coding tasks, as clearly illustrated in Figure 4.5. On code-centric evaluations such as LiveCodeBench, Codeforces, SWE-Bench, and Aider Polyglot, DeepSeek R1 consistently outperforms established models like Claude 3.5-Sonnet and GPT-4o, and is competitive with or surpasses OpenAI's most advanced offerings. For example, DeepSeek R1 achieves a LiveCodeBench Pass@1 COT score of 65.9, notably higher than Claude 3.5-Sonnet (33.8) and GPT-4o (24.2), and marginally ahead of OpenAI 01-preview (63.4).

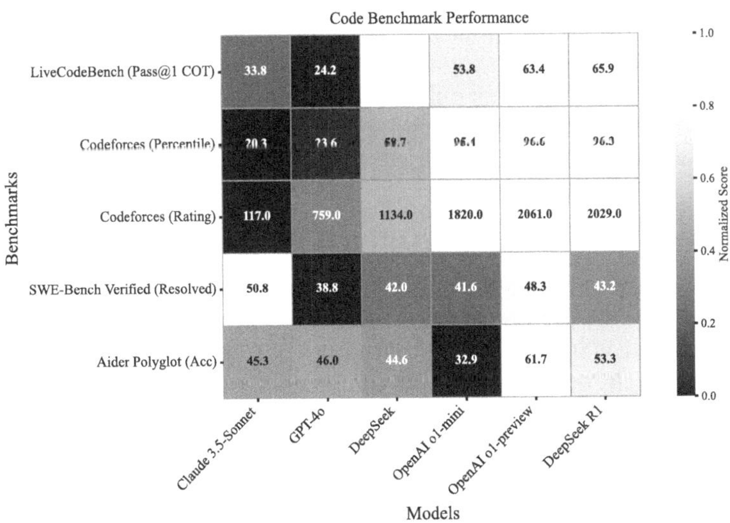

Figure 4.5 Comparative model performance on coding tasks.

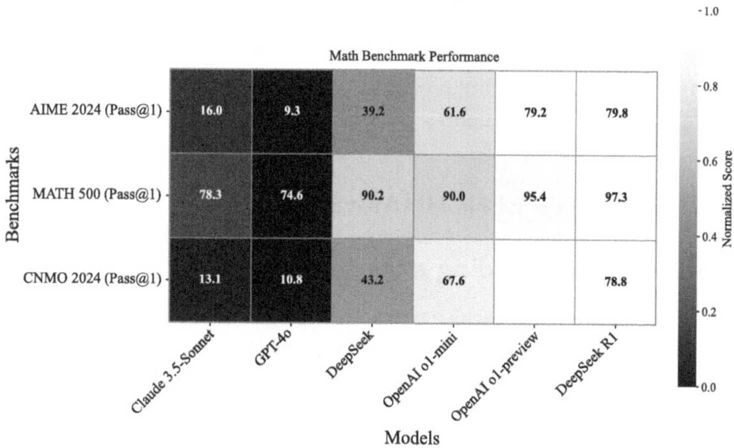

Figure 4.6 Comparative model performance on math and reasoning.

In terms of mathematical reasoning, DeepSeek models also shine, as shown in Figure 4.6. On datasets like MATH 500 and CNMO 2024, DeepSeek R1 delivers a Pass@1 score of 97.3 on MATH 500 and 78.8 on CNMO 2024, outperforming Claude 3.5-Sonnet and GPT-4o by a substantial margin and closely tracking the performance of OpenAI's top-tier models. These results underscore DeepSeek's strength not only in natural language understanding but also in complex symbolic and quantitative reasoning, an increasingly critical competency for advanced AI agents.

Multilingual and cross-cultural excellence

DeepSeek's multilingual and cross-cultural excellence is validated by its performance on Chinese benchmarks (Figure 4.7). On CLUEWSC and C Eval, DeepSeek R1 scores 92.8 and 91.8, respectively, outperforming all competitors, including OpenAI and Anthropic models. DeepSeek R1 achieves top scores on CLUEWSC and C-Eval, surpassing leading competitors such as OpenAI and Anthropic models. These results highlight DeepSeek's multilingual and cross-cultural excellence, demonstrating robust reasoning, coding, and language capabilities across diverse linguistic domains. Benchmark results demonstrate DeepSeek's architecture is well-optimised for reasoning, coding, and language tasks across multiple domains and languages.

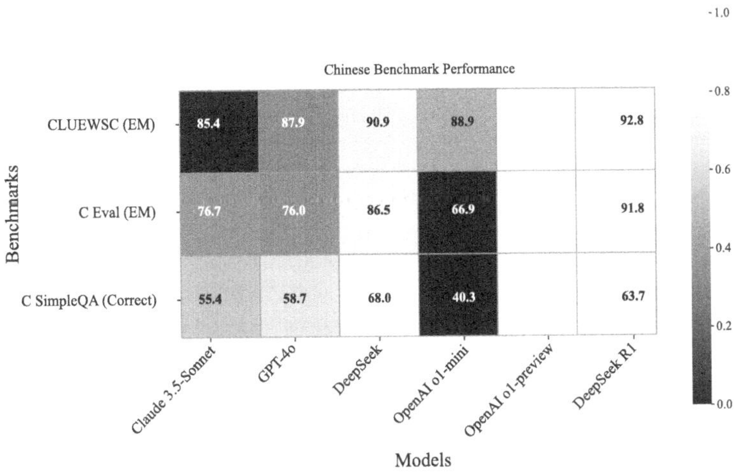

Figure 4.7 DeepSeek R1's performance on Chinese language benchmarks.

CONCLUSION

DeepSeek's unique blend of open-source philosophy, reasoning-centric design, and resource-efficient architecture has enabled it to achieve remarkable cost-to-performance ratios. Its performances often surpass leading Western models in both specialised and multilingual benchmarks. DeepSeek R1 focuses on transparent logic, empathetic responsiveness, and broad linguistic adaptability to advance the technical frontier. Its rapid evolution and disruptive results in reasoning, coding, and cross-cultural understanding signal a new paradigm for AI innovation. From the broader LLM perspective, DeepSeek exemplifies how targeted architectural choices, and open collaboration can drive not just incremental progress, but also transformative shifts in the way large language models are developed, deployed, and democratised worldwide.

REFERENCES

Baptista, E. (2025, January 28). Explainer: What is DeepSeek and why is it disrupting the AI sector? Ruters. https://www.reuters.com/technology/artificial-intelligence/what-is-deepseek-why-is-it-disrupting-ai-sector-2025-01-27/

Dahlke, R., Klagges, H., Zecha, D., Merkel, B., Rohr, S., & Klemm, F. (2025). *Mixture of Tunable Experts—Behavior Modification of DeepSeek-R1 at Inference Time* (No. arXiv:2502.11096). arXiv. https://doi.org/10.48550/arXiv.2502.11096

Dai, D., Deng, C., Zhao, C., Xu, R. X., Gao, H., Chen, D., Li, J., Zeng, W., Yu, X., Wu, Y., Xie, Z., Li, Y. K., Huang, P., Luo, F., Ruan, C., Sui, Z., & Liang, W. (2024). *DeepSeekMoE: Towards Ultimate Expert Specialization in Mixture-of-Experts Language Models* (No. arXiv:2401.06066). arXiv. https://doi.org/10.48550/arXiv.2401.06066

DeepSeek-AI, Bi, X., Chen, D., Chen, G., Chen, S., Dai, D., Deng, C., Ding, H., Dong, K., Du, Q., Fu, Z., Gao, H., Gao, K., Gao, W., Ge, R., Guan, K., Guo, D., Guo, J., Hao, G., … Zou, Y. (2024). *DeepSeek LLM: Scaling Open-Source Language Models with Longtermism* (No. arXiv:2401.02954). arXiv. https://doi.org/10.48550/arXiv.2401.02954

DeepSeek-AI, Guo, D., Yang, D., Zhang, H., Song, J., Zhang, R., Xu, R., Zhu, Q., Ma, S., Wang, P., Bi, X., Zhang, X., Yu, X., Wu, Y., Wu, Z. F., Gou, Z., Shao, Z., Li, Z., Gao, Z., … Zhang, Z. (2025). *DeepSeek-R1: Incentivizing Reasoning Capability in LLMs via Reinforcement Learning* (No. arXiv:2501.12948). arXiv. https://doi.org/10.48550/arXiv.2501.12948

DeepSeek-AI, Liu, A., Feng, B., Xue, B., Wang, B., Wu, B., Lu, C., Zhao, C., Deng, C., Zhang, C., Ruan, C., Dai, D., Guo, D., Yang, D., Chen, D., Ji, D., Li, E., Lin, F., Dai, F., … Pan, Z. (2025). *DeepSeek-V3 Technical Report* (No. arXiv:2412.19437). arXiv. https://doi.org/10.48550/arXiv.2412.19437

DeepSeek-AI, Zhu, Q., Guo, D., Shao, Z., Yang, D., Wang, P., Xu, R., Wu, Y., Li, Y., Gao, H., Ma, S., Zeng, W., Bi, X., Gu, Z., Xu, H., Dai, D., Dong, K., Zhang, L., Piao, Y., … Liang, W. (2024). *DeepSeek-Coder-V2: Breaking the Barrier of Closed-Source Models in Code Intelligence* (No. arXiv:2406.11931). arXiv. https://doi.org/10.48550/arXiv.2406.11931

Deepseek-ai/DeepSeek-R1 · Hugging Face. (2025, May 29). https://huggingface.co/deepseek-ai/DeepSeek-R1

Deepseek-ai/DeepSeek-R1-Zero · Hugging Face. (2025, May 29. https://huggingface.co/deepseek-ai/DeepSeek-R1-Zero

Deng, Z., Ma, W., Han, Q.-L., Zhou, W., Zhu, X., Wen, S., & Xiang, Y. (2025). Exploring DeepSeek: A Survey on Advances, Applications, Challenges and Future Directions. *IEEE/CAA Journal of Automatica Sinica*, *12*(5), 872–893. https://doi.org/10.1109/JAS.2025.125498

Dong, G., Yuan, H., Lu, K., Li, C., Xue, M., Liu, D., Wang, W., Yuan, Z., Zhou, C., & Zhou, J. (2024). *How Abilities in Large Language Models are Affected by Supervised Fine-tuning Data Composition* (No. arXiv:2310.05492). arXiv. https://doi.org/10.48550/arXiv.2310.05492

Huang, D., & Wang, Z. (2025). *Explainable Sentiment Analysis with DeepSeek-R1: Performance, Efficiency, and Few-Shot Learning* (No. arXiv:2503.11655). arXiv. https://doi.org/10.48550/arXiv.2503.11655

Li, Z.-Z., Zhang, D., Zhang, M.-L., Zhang, J., Liu, Z., Yao, Y., Xu, H., Zheng, J., Wang, P.-J., Chen, X., Zhang, Y., Yin, F., Dong, J., Li, Z., Bi, B.-L., Mei, L.-R., Fang, J., Liang, X., Guo, Z., … Liu, C.-L. (2025). *From System 1 to System 2: A Survey of Reasoning Large Language Models* (No. arXiv:2502.17419). arXiv. https://doi.org/10.48550/arXiv.2502.17419

Mercer, S., Spillard, S., & Martin, D. P. (2025). *Brief analysis of DeepSeek R1 and its implications for Generative AI* (No. arXiv:2502.02523). arXiv. https://doi.org/10.48550/arXiv.2502.02523

Park, C., Kim, J., Lee, J., Bae, S., Choo, J., & Yoo, K. M. (2025). *Cross-lingual Collapse: How Language-Centric Foundation Models Shape Reasoning in Large Language Models* (No. arXiv:2506.05850). arXiv. https://doi.org/10.48550/arXiv.2506.05850

Peng, H., Qi, Y., Wang, X., Yao, Z., Xu, B., Hou, L., & Li, J. (2025). *Agentic Reward Modeling: Integrating Human Preferences with Verifiable Correctness Signals for Reliable Reward Systems* (No. arXiv: 2502.19328). arXiv. https://doi.org/10.48550/arXiv.2502.19328

Puspitasari, F. D., Zhang, C., Dam, S. K., Zhang, M., Kim, T.-H., Hong, C. S., Bae, S.-H., Qin, C., Wei, J., Wang, G., & Yang, Y. (2025). *DeepSeek Models: A Comprehensive Survey of Methods and Applications*. https://doi.org/10.13140/RG.2.2.14903.43688

Rasool, A., Shahzad, M. I., Aslam, H., Chan, V., & Arshad, M. A. (2025). Emotion-Aware Embedding Fusion in Large Language Models (Flan-T5, Llama 2, DeepSeek-R1, and ChatGPT 4) for Intelligent Response Generation. *AI*, *6*(3), 56. https://doi.org/10.3390/ai6030056

Sallam, M., Al-Mahzoum, K., Sallam, M., & Mijwil, M. M. (2025). DeepSeek: Is it the End of Generative AI Monopoly or the Mark of the Impending Doomsday? *Mesopotamian Journal of Big Data*, *2025*, 26–34. https://doi.org/10.58496/MJBD/2025/002

Shao, Z., Wang, P., Zhu, Q., Xu, R., Song, J., Bi, X., Zhang, H., Zhang, M., Li, Y. K., Wu, Y., & Guo, D. (2024). *DeepSeekMath: Pushing the Limits of Mathematical Reasoning in Open Language Models* (No. arXiv:2402.03300). arXiv. https://doi.org/10.48550/arXiv.2402.03300

Singh, S., Bansal, S., Saddik, A. E., & Saini, M. (2025). *From ChatGPT to DeepSeek AI: A Comprehensive Analysis of Evolution, Deviation, and Future Implications in AI-Language Models* (No. arXiv:2504.03219). arXiv. https://doi.org/10.48550/arXiv.2504.03219

Tang, Y., Yang, Y., & Abbasi, A. (2025). *PersonaFuse: A Personality Activation-Driven Framework for Enhancing Human-LLM Interactions* (No. arXiv:2509.07370). arXiv. https://doi.org/10.48550/arXiv.2509.07370

Xiang, V., Snell, C., Gandhi, K., Albalak, A., Singh, A., Blagden, C., Phung, D., Rafailov, R., Lile, N., Mahan, D., Castricato, L., Franken, J.-P., Haber, N., & Finn, C. (2025). *Towards System 2 Reasoning in LLMs: Learning How to Think With Meta Chain-of-Thought* (No. arXiv:2501.04682). arXiv. https://doi.org/10.48550/arXiv.2501.04682

Zhao, C., Deng, C., Ruan, C., Dai, D., Gao, H., Li, J., Zhang, L., Huang, P., Zhou, S., Ma, S., Liang, W., He, Y., Wang, Y., Liu, Y., & Wei, Y. X. (2025). Insights into DeepSeek-V3: Scaling Challenges and Reflections on Hardware for AI Architectures. *Proceedings of the 52nd Annual International Symposium on Computer Architecture*, 1731–1745. https://doi.org/10.1145/3695053.3731412

Chapter 5

Transforming mental health with DeepSeek

M. W. Geda and Yuk Ming Tang

INTRODUCTION

Mental health disorders represent one of the most significant yet frequently overlooked public health challenges of the modern era (Mills, 2018). According to a report by World Health Organisation, globally, mental illness affects a substantial proportion of the population, with recent estimates indicating that nearly one in eight people live with a diagnosable mental disorder (Organization, 2022; Shen et al., 2024). Mental illness affects everyone equally, with high prevalence even among groups typically considered physically healthy (Grant et al., 2018). Mental health issues extend far beyond prevalence rates: they contribute to considerable personal suffering, reduced quality of life, social exclusion, and substantial economic losses at both individual and societal levels.

Despite the high prevalence and significant burden of mental health disorders, access to effective care remains limited for the majority of those affected (Lattie et al., 2022). Recent data highlights substantial delays in traditional mental health care delivery, with 23% of individuals with mental illnesses waiting over 12 weeks for face-to-face psychotherapy sessions, 12% waiting more than 6 months, and 6% enduring delays exceeding a year (Gregory, 2022). Nearly 43% of adults with mental illnesses reported their conditions worsened as a result of these delays (Gregory, 2022). This is due to a confluence of barriers, such as critical shortages of trained professionals, inadequate infrastructure, and prohibitive costs, which collectively restrict service availability and quality (Organization, 2022). Compounding these structural issues, pervasive stigma and discrimination frequently prevent people from seeking help (Peter et al., 2021). Cultural factors including diverse belief systems, and

 DOI: 10.1201/9781003649137-7

languages related to mental health shape how individuals recognise their own or others' distress and influence their decisions on whether, and where, to seek support (Zhang et al., 2021).

Amid these challenges, advances in artificial intelligence (AI) particularly the emergence of large language models (LLMs) such as DeepSeek have opened new avenues for mental health support and intervention (van Heerden et al., 2023). DeepSeek, powered by cutting-edge natural language processing and generative AI (Gen AI), excels at understanding and generating human-like responses in multiple languages, including Mandarin, enabling accessible and immediate support tailored to Chinese society (Zhu et al., 2024). With its scalable, cost-effective architecture and capabilities in processing diverse data, DeepSeek has the potential to enhance clinicians' capacities, deliver timely and tailored mental health interventions, and address barriers such as geographic isolation and linguistic diversity (Joshi, 2025). Additionally, DeepSeek's ability to process real-time data and operate offline for privacy-sensitive settings positions it to potentially support early detection, efficient triage, and continuous monitoring, thereby helping to address critical gaps in the mental health care (Temsah et al., 2025).

This chapter is organised to guide the reader from the urgent need for innovation in mental health care to the practical and technological dimensions of deploying large language models, particularly DeepSeek. We begin by framing the critical challenges that persist in mental health service delivery and the opportunities presented by recent advances in artificial intelligence. Next, we discuss how LLMs are applied across key domains in mental health, including education, diagnosis, conversational support, intervention planning, and care accessibility. Special emphasis is placed on DeepSeek's potential to provide empathetic, transparent, and culturally sensitive support. Throughout the chapter, we integrate both the foundational technological aspects and the real-world implications of using DeepSeek, concluding with reflections on its current role and future promise in digital mental health care.

GENERATIVE AI AND LLMS IN MENTAL HEALTH SUPPORT

The integration of GenAI and LLMs is rapidly transforming the landscape of mental health support. These technologies enable scalable, accessible, and contextually adaptive interventions that can augment traditional care and extend support to underserved populations. This section explores the core capabilities and challenges of LLMs, the application of Gen AI and natural language processing (NLP) for empathetic engagement, the critical role of sentiment and emotion analysis in personalising digital counselling, and the importance of transparency in fostering trust in AI-driven mental health tools.

LLM-DRIVEN DIGITAL MENTAL HEALTH SOLUTIONS

LLMs represent a significant breakthrough in natural language understanding, allowing machines to interpret and generate complex human language with a high degree of fluency (Huang et al., 2025). In mental health applications, LLMs can assist with symptom screening, provide psychoeducation, and offer supportive dialogue tailored to individual user needs (Ni & Jia, 2025). The advent of models such as GPT-3, LLaMA, GPT-4, and DeepSeek has further revolutionised tasks such as generative question answering, enabling fluent, and contextually relevant responses even in specialised domains such as medical QA (Ji et al., 2023). These models, constructed with billions of parameters and trained on massive and diverse text corpora, can identify and reproduce intricate patterns in human language (Minaee et al., 2025). Figure 5.1 illustrates the core domains where LLMs can be applied to mental health support, including accessibility and efficiency, mental health education, diagnosis and screening, conversational support, and intervention planning. Representative models, application modalities, target users, and open-source resources for each domain are summarised in Table 5.1.

ENHANCING MENTAL HEALTH LITERACY WITH LLMS

Mental health education has been one of the most promising areas for LLM application. Large Language Models, when appropriately developed and deployed, can significantly expand access to evidence-based mental health information and support, addressing

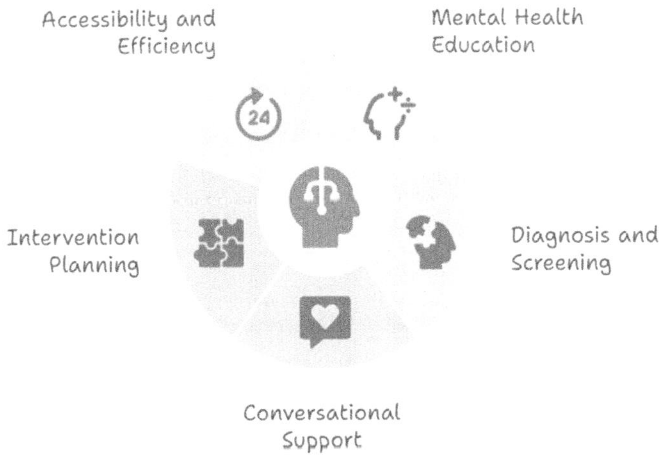

Figure 5.1 Core application domains of LLMs in mental health support.

some of the pressing global gaps in mental health literacy and service provision (Lawrence et al., 2024). Studies indicate that LLMs such as DeepSeek provide psychoeducation with empathy, making them particularly useful for individuals with limited access to traditional mental health resources (Kelly Ng, 2025). Moreover, they consistently incorporate ethical guidance, such as advising users to seek professional help where appropriate, and engage users through actionable and supportive responses. Moreover, they demonstrate significant effort to incorporate ethical guidance, such as advising users to seek professional help where appropriate (Maurya et al., 2025). Targeted approaches, such as chatbots tailored for adolescents, have further demonstrated the potential of LLMs to raise awareness and foster open dialogue about mental health disorders in sensitive populations (Mármol-Romero et al., 2025).

In clinical training, LLMs can serve as simulated patients, enabling medical students to practice history-taking and communication skills in a low-stress, repeatable environment (De Duro et al., 2025). These systems provide plausible and contextually relevant interactions, supporting the development of essential communication competencies, although occasional lapses into socially desirable or less medically plausible responses have been noted (A Generative Pretrained Transformer (GPT)–Powered Chatbot as a Simulated Patient to Practice History Taking: Prospective, Mixed Methods Study, 2024). Beyond simulated interactions, LLMs such as ChatGPT

Table 5.1 Representative LLM applications in digital mental health, categorised by functional domain

Ref.	*Application category*	*LLM model*	*Modality*	*Language*	*Target user*	*Open-source*
(Lawrence et al., 2024), (Maurya et al., 2025), (Mármol-Romero et al., 2025), (Holderried et al., , 2024), (Gilson et al., 2023)	Mental health education	ChatGPT, GPT-3, GPT-3.5, InstructGPT	Text, Text (Chatbot), Text (QA)	English, Spanish	General public, Teenagers, Medical students	• https://chatgpt.com • https://platform.openai.com
(Elyoseph et al., 2024), (Levkovich, 2025), (Franco D'Souza et al., 2023), (Chopra et al., 2024), (Xu et al., 2024),	Diagnostic, Assessment, and screening	Roberta, BERT, GPT-3.5, Gemini 2.0, Claude 3.5, ChatGPT-4, Alpaca,	Text, Text (chatbot)	English	General public, Professionals	• https://gemini.google.com • https://huggingface.co/docs/transformers/en/model_doc/roberta • https://huggingface.co/docs/transformers/en/model_doc/bert • https://github.com/tatsu-lab/stanford_alpaca

(Adhikary et al., 2024; De Duro et al., 2025), (Berrezueta-Guzman et al., 2024), (Adhikary et al., 2024), (Yang et al., 2024), (Wang et al., 2024), (Wang et al., 2024),	Conversational support and Counselling	Mistral, MentalLlama, MentalBART, ClientCAST	Text (chatbot)	English, Italian	General public, Professionals	• https://huggingface.co/Tianlin668/MentalBART • https://mistral.ai • https://github.com/SteveKGYang/MentalLLaMA • https://github.com/wangjs9/ClientCAST
(Nie et al., 2024), (Wilhelm et al., 2023), (Wei et al., 2023), (Elyoseph et al., 2024), (Huang et al., 2024), (Stade et al., 2024),	Intervention and treatment Planning	CaiTI (LLM-based Conversational AI Therapist), Claude-instant-v1.0, GPT-3.5-Turbo, Command-xlarge-nightly, Bloomz, ChatGPT	Text (chatbot), Text (recommendation), Text (screening)	English	General public, Professionals, Psychiatry Patients	• https://docs.anthropic.com/en/docs.about-claude/models/overview • https://docs.cohere.com/changelog/command-model-nightly-available • https://huggingface.co/bigscience/bloomz
(Stade et al., 2024), (Kung et al., 2023), (Gilson et al., 2023, Kitamura, 2023), (Koltcov et al., 2024)	Accessibility and efficiency in care delivery	GPT-4, DeepSeek, LLMs (fine-tuned)	Text, Text (annotation), Text (triage)	English	General public, Medical students, Clinicians	• https://platform.openai.com • https://www.deepseek.com

have also shown strong performance on standardised medical exams, achieving scores comparable to passing human candidates. Notably, these models provide logical justifications and contextual information in their answers, reinforcing their promise as interactive educational tools for both knowledge assessment and skill development (Gilson et al., 2023). State-of-the-art advancements show LLMs hold immense potential to enhance mental health education accessibility, yet they necessitate ongoing evaluation, targeted fine-tuning, and strong ethical oversight to maximise benefits and minimise risks.

LLM-ASSISTED DIAGNOSIS, ASSESSMENT, AND SCREENING

LLMs have demonstrated substantial promise in supporting the diagnosis, assessment, and screening of mental health conditions by providing rapid, scalable, and evidence-informed clinical decision support. Recent comparative studies highlight that LLMs such as ChatGPT-3.5, ChatGPT-4, Claude, Gemini, and Bard are capable of accurately identifying primary psychiatric diagnoses, such as depression, and often recommend guideline-concordant treatments including psychotherapy and pharmacotherapy (Elyoseph et al., 2024),(Levkovich, 2025). Notably, LLMs have matched or even surpassed mental health professionals in diagnostic accuracy for certain conditions, including depression, social phobia, and PTSD, when tested using clinical vignettes. For instance, ChatGPT-4 achieved 100% diagnostic accuracy in these domains, although its performance was less robust in more complex presentations, such as early schizophrenia (Levkovich, 2025). In another large-scale evaluation using 100 psychiatric case vignettes, ChatGPT-3.5 was consistently rated highly by expert psychiatrists for its management strategies and diagnostic reasoning, with the majority of its responses receiving excellent assessments and no critical errors in clinical care identified (Franco D'Souza et al., 2023).

Despite these advances, the integration of LLMs into diagnostic workflows requires careful oversight. While LLMs frequently recommend consulting healthcare professionals, their predictions about prognosis and recovery tend to be more conservative or even pessimistic compared to human experts (Elyoseph et al., 2024),(Levkovich, 2025). For example, earlier versions such as ChatGPT-3.5 sometimes offered negative prognoses that might

Figure 5.2 Contextual application of LLMs and trained professionals in the mental health diagnostic process.

dissuade users from seeking further care, while newer models more closely align with professional perspectives on the necessity of intervention and likely outcomes (Elyoseph et al., 2024). Furthermore, while LLMs provide valuable support for clinical decision-making and can help standardise initial assessments, they cannot replace the judgment and experience of trained professionals, especially in complex, and high-risk scenarios. As illustrated in Figure 5.2, LLMs and clinicians offer complementary strengths in the mental health diagnostic process. LLMs excel in rapid symptom screening, guideline recall, and scalable initial support, while human clinicians remain essential for complex case management, ethical adaptation, and high-risk decision-making. This balance underscores the value of integrating LLMs as adjuncts within clinical workflows, rather than as stand-alone replacements.

CONVERSATIONAL SUPPORT AND COUNSELLING WITH LLMS

The application of LLMs in conversational support and counselling represents a rapidly evolving area within digital mental health. LLMs are being used not only to facilitate supportive dialogue, but also to assist clinicians and clients by automating tasks such as

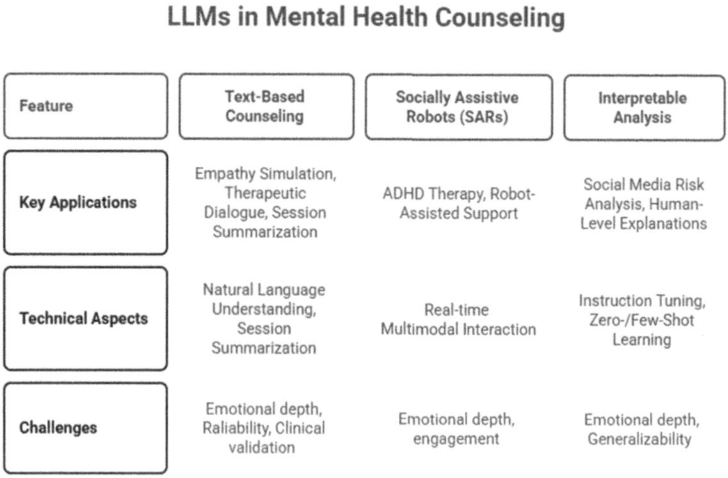

Figure 5.3 Overview of LLM applications in mental health counselling.

session summarisation, enhancing empathy, and supporting therapy planning (Adhikary et al., 2024). This technological landscape is diverse, spanning multiple modalities and technical approaches, each with unique opportunities and challenges. Figure 5.3 provides a comparative overview of the main domains where LLMs are currently deployed in mental health counselling. The diagram summarises key applications, technical aspects, and persistent challenges across these domains, highlighting both the breadth and complexity of LLM integration in counselling contexts.

Recent work has demonstrated that LLMs can generate concise and informative summaries of counselling sessions, which can support mental health professionals in maintaining continuity of care and optimising therapy planning (Qiu & Lan, 2024; Wang et al., 2025). Adhikary et al. (2024) benchmarked the performance of 11 state-of-the-art LLMs, including domain-specific models such as MentalLlama, Mistral, and MentalBART, for aspect-based summarisation of therapy sessions. Their findings indicate that while these specialised models outperform general purpose LLMs on automatic evaluation metrics, and Mistral in particular excelled in affective attitude, coherence, and ethicality, none yet achieve the reliability required for clinical deployment. The need for further refinement and validation of these models is underscored by expert assessments, especially regarding opportunity costs and perceived effectiveness.

With regard to simulating counselling conversations, De Duro et al. (2025) introduced CounseLLMe, a multilingual dataset comprising simulated mental health dialogues generated by LLMs such as GPT-3.5, Claude-3's Haiku, and LLaMAntino. Their analysis found that, in English, LLM-driven conversations can closely mimic the emotional and linguistic structure of real patient-therapist exchanges, particularly in terms of trust and empathy. Similarly, Wang et al. (2024) proposed ClientCAST, a client-centred approach to assess LLM therapists by simulating clients using LLMs. They simulated clients interact with LLM therapists to assess the capabilities and limitations of LLMs in therapeutic settings from the client's perspective. LLMs tend to miss certain negative emotions, such as anger and frustration, which are present in human conversations (Grandi et al., 2024). This suggests that while LLMs can realistically reproduce many aspects of counselling dialogue, capturing the full complexity of human emotional experience remains a challenge.

LLMs are also being integrated with socially assistive robots (SARs) to support therapy for specific populations (Kian et al., 2024). These robotic platforms enable more embodied and interactive therapeutic experiences, expanding the reach and effectiveness of digital interventions. Berrezueta-Guzman et al. (2024) evaluated robot-assisted interactions powered by ChatGPT-4 Turbo and Claude-3 Opus in the context of ADHD therapy. Their results indicate that LLMs can offer tailored and responsive support, with ChatGPT-4 Turbo excelling in speed and integration, and Claude-3 Opus performing best in coherence and ethical considerations. Further evidence of the promise of LLM-powered SARs comes from recent work by Kian et al. (2024), who developed a prompt-engineered SAR to guide university students through interactive cognitive behavioural therapy (CBT) exercises at home. Their findings reveal the SAR-guided group and the worksheet group both demonstrated significant reductions in general psychological distress over time, while the chatbot group did not. This suggest that LLM-driven SARs can deliver CBT in a manner that is at least as effective as traditional methods for longer-term outcomes, and potentially superior for promoting immediate therapeutic benefits and user engagement.

Efforts to enhance the interpretability and generalisability of LLMs for mental health counselling are underway. While LLMs show significant promise as conversation agents and counselling aides, enhancing empathy, automating clinical documentation, and supporting therapeutic engagement, further work is needed to address limitations related to emotional nuance, reliability, and clinical validation before they can be widely adopted in mental health practice. To this end, Yang et al. (2024) recently introduced MentaLLaMA, an open-source instruction-following LLM series developed for interpretable mental health analysis on social media. Using a large, expert-annotated dataset, MentaLLaMA achieved human-level explanations and strong performance across multiple tasks, demonstrating the potential for LLMs to provide both predictive and explanatory support in conversational mental health applications.

LLM-GUIDED INTERVENTION AND TREATMENT PLANNING

The integration of LLMs into intervention and treatment planning is an emerging frontier in digital mental health. LLMs offer the potential to support clinicians in designing, tailoring, and optimising therapeutic interventions for a wide range of mental health conditions (Wei et al., 2023). Recent developments have demonstrated that LLMs can analyse both structured and unstructured patient information, including clinical notes, patient histories, and self-reported symptoms to provide preliminary diagnostic suggestions and propose personalised treatment plans (Huang et al., 2024; Li et al., 2024). For example, Nie et al. (2024) introduced CaiTI, a conversational AI therapist platform leveraging LLMs and smart devices to facilitate psychotherapeutic screening and intervention in daily life. CaiTI can screen for day-to-day functioning through natural dialogue and deliver interventions such as cognitive behavioural therapy (CBT) and motivational interviewing (MI), with reinforcement learning enabling personalised conversation flows. In real-world studies, CaiTI demonstrated the ability to accurately interpret user responses and provide appropriate psychotherapeutic interventions, validated by licensed psychotherapists.

Comparative studies have evaluated the quality and safety of LLM-generated therapy recommendations across clinical specialties. Wilhelm et al. (2023) assessed multiple LLMs, finding significant differences in content quality, reliability, and safety. While some models, such as GPT-3.5-Turbo, were rated safest, others displayed lapses such as providing vague or incomplete advice, or omitting critical treatment options. Notably, the study introduced an auto-evaluation mechanism using GPT-4 to benchmark LLM responses against physician assessments, underscoring the need for continuous monitoring and refinement to ensure clinical safety and reliability. Moreover, LLMs are being explored to support ongoing monitoring and dynamic adjustment of treatment plans. By continuously analysing patient progress and feedback, LLMs can prompt timely modifications to therapeutic strategies or alert clinicians to signs of deterioration or crisis (Nie et al., 2024). Some applications also leverage LLMs to deliver psychoeducation, behavioural activation exercises directly to patients, further supporting engagement and adherence to treatment (Stade et al., 2024).

ACCESSIBILITY AND EFFICIENCY IN CARE DELIVERY

LLMs have the capability to automate parts of assessment, documentation, triage, and even certain psychotherapy elements, offering a promising approach to overcome systemic capacity constraints and enhance access to care for varied populations (Stade et al., 2024). One of the most significant promises of LLMs is their capacity to scale access to evidence-based information and interventions. For example, models such as GPT-4 and DeepSeek can provide on-demand, personalised psychoeducation and support, effectively extending the reach of mental health resources beyond the constraints of traditional clinical settings (Naik et al., 2025). This is particularly valuable in contexts where mental health professionals are scarce, or where stigma and logistical barriers inhibit help-seeking.

In medical education, LLMs have demonstrated an ability to perform at or near the passing threshold on standardised exams such as the United States Medical Licensing Examination (USMLE), suggesting their utility not only for augmenting professional training but also for supporting knowledge acquisition and clinical reasoning among trainees (Gilson et al., 2023; Kung et al., 2023). The capacity for these models to generate logical, interpretable rationales for their answers further enhances their potential as interactive educational tools and clinical decision-support systems.

Efficiency gains are also enabled by LLM-driven automation in data processing and annotation. For instance, Koltcov et al. (2024)

describe the use of LLMs to extract and pre-annotate large volumes of user-generated mental health texts from noisy, real-world data sources, including those in low-resource languages. Their work demonstrates that fine-tuned LLMs, especially when leveraging natural language inference (NLI) approaches, can substantially improve the quality and speed of classification and annotation tasks. This capability not only streamlines the development of mental health conversational agents for underserved linguistic communities but also reduces the manual burden on clinicians and annotators.

CONCLUSION

This chapter has examined the transformative role of DeepSeek and large language models in digital mental health care. We highlighted how DeepSeek enhances early detection, clinical decision support, and patient engagement, offering scalable and accessible solutions that complement traditional services. While technology brings notable benefits, such as improved reach, timely intervention, and personalised guidance, important challenges remain. Issues of bias, transparency, and clinical safety must be addressed through ongoing research, responsible deployment, and strong human oversight. As DeepSeek and similar models continue to evolve, they have the potential to make mental health care more inclusive, effective, and responsive to real-world needs.

REFERENCES

Holderried F., Stegemann-Philipps C., Herschbach L., Moldt J. A., Nevins A., Griewatz J., Holderried M., Herrmann-Werner A., Festl-Wietek T., Mahling M. (2024). A Generative Pretrained Transformer (GPT)–Powered Chatbot as a Simulated Patient to Practice History Taking: Prospective, Mixed Methods Study. *JMIR Medical Education, 10*. https://doi.org/10.2196/53961

Adhikary, P. K., Srivastava, A., Kumar, S., Singh, S. M., Manuja, P., Gopinath, J. K., Krishnan, V., Gupta, S. K., Deb, K. S., & Chakraborty, T. (2024). Exploring the Efficacy of Large Language Models in Summarizing Mental Health Counseling Sessions: Benchmark Study. *JMIR Mental Health*, *11*(1), e57306. https://doi.org/10.2196/57306

Berrezueta-Guzman, S., Kandil, M., Martín-Ruiz, M.-L., de la Cruz, I. P., & Krusche, S. (2024). Exploring the Efficacy of Robotic Assistants with ChatGPT and Claude in Enhancing ADHD Therapy: Innovating Treatment

Paradigms. *2024 International Conference on Intelligent Environments (IE)*, 25–32. https://doi.org/10.1109/IE61493.2024.10599903

Chopra, S., Agarwal, P., Ahmed, J., Biswas, S. S., & Obaid, A. J. (2024). Roberta and BERT: Revolutionizing Mental Healthcare Through Natural Language. *SN Computer Science*, *5*(7), 889. https://doi.org/10.1007/s42979-024-03202-8

De Duro, E. S., Improta, R., & Stella, M. (2025). Introducing CounseLLMe: A dataset of simulated mental health dialogues for comparing LLMs like Haiku, LLaMAntino and ChatGPT against humans. *Emerging Trends in Drugs, Addictions, and Health*, *5*, 100170. https://doi.org/10.1016/j.etdah.2025.100170

Elyoseph, Z., Levkovich, I., & Shinan-Altman, S. (2024). Assessing prognosis in depression: Comparing perspectives of AI models, mental health professionals and the general public. *Family Medicine and Community Health*, *12*(Suppl 1), e002583. https://doi.org/10.1136/fmch-2023-002583

Franco D'Souza, R., Amanullah, S., Mathew, M., & Surapaneni, K. M. (2023). Appraising the performance of ChatGPT in psychiatry using 100 clinical case vignettes. *Asian Journal of Psychiatry*, *89*, 103770. https://doi.org/10.1016/j.ajp.2023.103770

Gilson, A., Safranek, C. W., Huang, T., Socrates, V., Chi, L., Taylor, R. A., & Chartash, D. (2023). How Does ChatGPT Perform on the United States Medical Licensing Examination (USMLE)? The Implications of Large Language Models for Medical Education and Knowledge Assessment. *JMIR Medical Education*, *9*, e45312. https://doi.org/10.2196/45312

Grandi, A. D., Ravenda, F., Raballo, A., & Crestani, F. (2024). *The Emotional Spectrum of LLMs: Leveraging Empathy and Emotion-Based Markers for Mental Health Support* (No. arXiv:2412.20068). arXiv. https://doi.org/10.48550/arXiv.2412.20068

Grant, K. L., Simmons, M. B., & Davey, C. G. (2018). Three Nontraditional Approaches to Improving the Capacity, Accessibility, and Quality of Mental Health Services: An Overview. *Psychiatric Services*, *69*(5), 508–516. https://doi.org/10.1176/appi.ps.201700292

Gregory, A. (2022, October 10). Patients turning to A&E as wait times for NHS mental health treatment spiral. *The Guardian*. https://www.theguardian.com/society/2022/oct/10/nhs-mental-health-patients-wait-times

Huang, J., Yang, D. M., Rong, R., Nezafati, K., Treager, C., Chi, Z., Wang, S., Cheng, X., Guo, Y., Klesse, L. J., Xiao, G., Peterson, E. D., Zhan, X., & Xie, Y. (2024). A critical assessment of using ChatGPT for extracting structured data from clinical notes. *Npj Digital Medicine*, 7(1), 106. https://doi.org/10.1038/s41746-024-01079-8

Huang, L., Yu, W., Ma, W., Zhong, W., Feng, Z., Wang, H., Chen, Q., Peng, W., Feng, X., Qin, B., & Liu, T. (2025). A Survey on Hallucination in Large Language Models: Principles, Taxonomy, Challenges, and Open Questions. *ACM Transactions on Information Systems*, *43*(2), 1–55. https://doi.org/10.1145/3703155

Ji, Z., Yu, T., Xu, Y., Lee, N., Ishii, E., & Fung, P. (2023). *Towards Mitigating Hallucination in Large Language Models via Self-Reflection* (No. arXiv:2310.06271). arXiv. https://doi.org/10.48550/arXiv.2310.06271

Joshi, S. (2025). *A Comprehensive Review of DeepSeek: Performance, Architecture and Capabilities* (No. 2025031887). Preprints. https://doi.org/10.20944/preprints202503.1887.v1

Kian, M. J., Zong, M., Fischer, K., Singh, A., Velentza, A.-M., Sang, P., Upadhyay, S., Gupta, A., Faruki, M. A., Browning, W., Arnold, S. M. R., Krishnamachari, B., & Mataric, M. J. (2024). *Can an LLM-Powered Socially Assistive Robot Effectively and Safely Deliver Cognitive Behavioral Therapy? A Study With University Students* (No. arXiv:2402.17937). arXiv. https://doi.org/10.48550/arXiv.2402.17937

Kitamura, F. C. (2023). ChatGPT Is Shaping the Future of Medical Writing But Still Requires Human Judgment. *Radiology*, *307*(2), e230171. https://doi.org/10.1148/radiol.230171

Koltcov, S., Surkov, A., Koltsova, O., & Ignatenko, V. (2024). Using large language models for extracting and pre-annotating texts on mental health from noisy data in a low-resource language. *PeerJ Computer Science*, *10*, e2395. https://doi.org/10.7717/peerj-cs.2395

Kung, T. H., Cheatham, M., Medenilla, A., Sillos, C., Leon, L. D., Elepaño, C., Madriaga, M., Aggabao, R., Diaz-Candido, G., Maningo, J., & Tseng, V. (2023). Performance of ChatGPT on USMLE: Potential for AI-assisted medical education using large language models. *PLOS Digital Health*, *2*(2), e0000198. https://doi.org/10.1371/journal.pdig.0000198

Lattie, E. G., Stiles-Shields, C., & Graham, A. K. (2022). An overview of and recommendations for more accessible digital mental health services. *Nature Reviews Psychology*, *1*(2), 87–100. https://doi.org/10.1038/s44159-021-00003-1

Lawrence, H. R., Schneider, R. A., Rubin, S. B., Matarić, M. J., McDuff, D. J., & Bell, M. J. (2024). The Opportunities and Risks of Large Language Models in Mental Health. *JMIR Mental Health*, *11*(1), e59479. https://doi.org/10.2196/59479

Levkovich, I. (2025). Evaluating Diagnostic Accuracy and Treatment Efficacy in Mental Health: A Comparative Analysis of Large Language Model Tools and Mental Health Professionals. *European Journal of Investigation in Health, Psychology and Education*, *15*(1), 9. https://doi.org/10.3390/ejihpe15010009

Li, L., Zhou, J., Gao, Z., Hua, W., Fan, L., Yu, H., Hagen, L., Zhang, Y., Assimes, T. L., Hemphill, L., & Ma, S. (2024). *A scoping review of using Large Language Models (LLMs) to investigate Electronic Health Records (EHRs)* (No. arXiv:2405.03066). arXiv. https://doi.org/10.48550/arXiv.2405.03066

Mármol-Romero, A. M., García-Vega, M., García-Cumbreras, M. Á., & Montejo-Ráez, A. (2025). An Empathic GPT-Based Chatbot to Talk

About Mental Disorders With Spanish Teenagers. *International Journal of Human–Computer Interaction*, *41*(7), 3957–3973. https://doi.org/10.1080/10447318.2024.2344355

Maurya, R. K., Montesinos, S., Bogomaz, M., & DeDiego, A. C. (2025). Assessing the use of ChatGPT as a psychoeducational tool for mental health practice. *Counselling and Psychotherapy Research*, *25*(1), e12759. https://doi.org/10.1002/capr.12759

Mills, C. (2018). From 'Invisible Problem' to Global Priority: The Inclusion of Mental Health in the Sustainable Development Goals. *Development and Change*, *49*(3), 843–866. https://doi.org/10.1111/dech.12397

Minaee, S., Mikolov, T., Nikzad, N., Chenaghlu, M., Socher, R., Amatriain, X., & Gao, J. (2025). *Large Language Models: A Survey* (No. arXiv:2402.06196). arXiv. https://doi.org/10.48550/arXiv.2402.06196

Naik, A., Thomas, J., Sree, T., & Reddy, H. (2025). *Artificial Empathy: AI based Mental Health* (No. arXiv:2506.00081). arXiv. https://doi.org/10.48550/arXiv.2506.00081

Ng, K. (2025, February 12). *"DeepSeek brought me to tears": How young Chinese find therapy in AI*. https://www.bbc.com/news/articles/cy7g45g2nxno

Ni, Y., & Jia, F. (2025). A Scoping Review of AI-Driven Digital Interventions in Mental Health Care: Mapping Applications Across Screening, Support, Monitoring, Prevention, and Clinical Education. *Healthcare*, *13*(10), 1205. https://doi.org/10.3390/healthcare13101205

Nie, J., Shao, H., Fan, Y., Shao, Q., You, H., Preindl, M., & Jiang, X. (2024). *LLM-based Conversational AI Therapist for Daily Functioning Screening and Psychotherapeutic Intervention via Everyday Smart Devices* (No. arXiv:2403.10779). arXiv. https://doi.org/10.48550/arXiv.2403.10779

Organization (2022). *World mental health report: Transforming mental health for all*. World Health Organization.

Peter, L.-J., Schindler, S., Sander, C., Schmidt, S., Muehlan, H., McLaren, T., Tomczyk, S., Speerforck, S., & Schomerus, G. (2021). Continuum beliefs and mental illness stigma: A systematic review and meta-analysis of correlation and intervention studies. *Psychological Medicine*, *51*(5), 716–726. https://doi.org/10.1017/S0033291721000854

Qiu, H., & Lan, Z. (2024). *Interactive Agents: Simulating Counselor-Client Psychological Counseling via Role-Playing LLM-to-LLM Interactions* (No. arXiv:2408.15787). arXiv. https://doi.org/10.48550/arXiv.2408.15787

Shen, N., Jilka, S., & Sawchuk, K. (2024). Editorial: World mental health day 2022: key drivers of risk to mental health services and innovative solutions. *Frontiers in Health Services*, *4*. https://doi.org/10.3389/frhs.2024.1456603

Stade, E. C., Stirman, S. W., Ungar, L. H., Boland, C. L., Schwartz, H. A., Yaden, D. B., Sedoc, J., DeRubeis, R. J., Willer, R., & Eichstaedt, J. C. (2024). Large language models could change the future of behavioral healthcare: A proposal for responsible development and evaluation. *Npj Mental Health Research*, *3*(1), 12. https://doi.org/10.1038/s44184-024-00056-z

Temsah, A., Alhasan, K., Altamimi, I., Jamal, A., Al-Eyadhy, A., Malki, K. H., & Temsah, M.-H. (2025). DeepSeek in Healthcare: Revealing Opportunities and Steering Challenges of a New Open-Source Artificial Intelligence Frontier. *Cureus*, *17*(2), e79221. https://doi.org/10.7759/cureus.79221

van Heerden, A. C., Pozuelo, J. R., & Kohrt, B. A. (2023). Global Mental Health Services and the Impact of Artificial Intelligence–Powered Large Language Models. *JAMA Psychiatry*, *80*(7), 662–664. https://doi.org/10.1001/jamapsychiatry.2023.1253

Wang, J., Xiao, Y., Li, Y., Song, C., Xu, C., Tan, C., & Li, W. (2024). *Towards a Client-Centered Assessment of LLM Therapists by Client Simulation* (No. arXiv:2406.12266). arXiv. https://doi.org/10.48550/arXiv.2406.12266

Wang, Y., Wang, Y., Xiao, Y., Escamilla, L., Augustine, B., Crace, K., Zhou, G., & Zhang, Y. (2025). *Evaluating an LLM-Powered Chatbot for Cognitive Restructuring: Insights from Mental Health Professionals* (No. arXiv:2501.15599). arXiv. https://doi.org/10.48550/arXiv.2501.15599

Wei, Y., Guo, L., Lian, C., & Chen, J. (2023). ChatGPT: Opportunities, risks and priorities for psychiatry. *Asian Journal of Psychiatry*, *90*, 103808. https://doi.org/10.1016/j.ajp.2023.103808

Wilhelm, T. I., Roos, J., & Kaczmarczyk, R. (2023). Large Language Models for Therapy Recommendations Across 3 Clinical Specialties: Comparative Study. *Journal of Medical Internet Research*, *25*(1), e49324. https://doi.org/10.2196/49324

Xu, X., Yao, B., Dong, Y., Gabriel, S., Yu, H., Hendler, J., Ghassemi, M., Dey, A. K., & Wang, D. (2024). Mental-LLM: Leveraging Large Language Models for Mental Health Prediction via Online Text Data. *Proceedings of the ACM on Interactive, Mobile, Wearable and Ubiquitous Technologies*, *8*(1), 1–31. https://doi.org/10.1145/3643540

Yang, K., Zhang, T., Kuang, Z., Xie, Q., Huang, J., & Ananiadou, S. (2024). MentaLLaMA: Interpretable Mental Health Analysis on Social Media with Large Language Models. *Proceedings of the ACM Web Conference 2024*, 4489–4500. https://doi.org/10.1145/3589334.3648137

Zhang, X., Lewis, S., Firth, J., Chen, X., & Bucci, S. (2021). Digital mental health in China: A systematic review. *Psychological Medicine*, *51*(15), 2552–2570. https://doi.org/10.1017/S0033291721003731

Zhu, S., Supryadi, Xu, S., Sun, H., Pan, L., Cui, M., Du, J., Jin, R., Branco, A., & Xiong, D. (2024). *Multilingual Large Language Models: A Systematic Survey* (No. arXiv:2411.11072). arXiv. https://doi.org/10.48550/arXiv.2411.11072

Chapter 6

Case studies: Real-life applications of DeepSeek

M. W. Geda and Yuk Ming Tang

INTRODUCTION

The rapid evolution of artificial intelligence (AI) is transforming mental health care, opening new avenues for accessible, scalable, and personalised support (Babu & Joseph, 2024). Among these advances, large language models (LLMs) are at the forefront, capable of interpreting human emotions and providing both practical assistance and empathetic engagement (Naik et al., 2025; Sorin et al., 2024). DeepSeek, a state-of-the-art LLM platform, exemplifies this shift by delivering digital emotional support and robust clinical decision assistance in real-world mental health settings (Sandmann et al., 2025). At its core, DeepSeek's design approach prioritises resource optimisation, enabling high-performance models with reduced computational demands and lower development costs compared to industry giants (Hong & Hu, 2025). This philosophy stems from a need to democratise advanced AI, making it viable for diverse applications without excessive resource barriers. Early influences include building on scalable architectures to address real-world challenges such as reasoning and efficiency, positioning DeepSeek as a disruptor in global AI landscapes (Sallam et al., 2025).

The importance of understanding DeepSeek's real-world impact cannot be overstated. Globally, mental health challenges are rising, yet millions continue to lack timely and effective care due to persistent shortages of professionals, widespread stigma, and systemic barriers (Organization, 2022; Sorin et al., 2024). Against this backdrop, DeepSeek's ability to provide confidential, 24/7 emotional support and to equip clinicians with evidence-based recommendations represents a significant advance for the field (Zhou et al., 2025).

DOI: 10.1201/9781003649137-8

DeepSeek's applications span a wide spectrum of use cases. For instance, young adults in China, facing growing mental health pressures, have turned to DeepSeek for confidential, round-the-clock emotional counselling when traditional resources are unavailable (Kelly, 2025; Zeng et al., 2025). Clinicians can also leverage DeepSeek to synthesise patient data, clinical guidelines, and biomedical literature, enabling more informed decisions in complex diagnostic and treatment scenarios (Zhou et al., 2025). Notably, DeepSeek's open-source framework, seamless integration with healthcare records, and transparent chain-of-thought reasoning distinguish it from other LLMs in the mental health domain (Ye et al., 2025).

However, the integration of AI-driven emotional support into mental health care is not without significant challenges. Issues such as model bias—where the system may inadvertently perpetuate existing societal prejudices, along with limited explainability and the need for culturally sensitive responses, underscore the complexity of deploying large language models in this sensitive domain (Deng et al., 2025; Sorin et al., 2024). Recognising these complexities is crucial when evaluating DeepSeek's real-world impact.

This chapter explores case studies and applications of DeepSeek to provide a window into not only the opportunities, but also the practical limitations and ethical considerations encountered in practice. The chapter explores how DeepSeek is being used to support individuals and clinicians, what benefits and limitations have emerged, and how ethical and technical challenges are encountered and addressed. Through analysis of system workflows and user experiences, this chapter provides an in-depth look at DeepSeek's real-world impact, offering insights that can inform future innovation and responsible implementation of AI in mental health care.

DEEPSEEK FOR EARLY DETECTION AND DIGITAL TRIAGE APPLICATION

Recent studies and reports indicate a rising prevalence of depression and anxiety among young adults in China, driven by socio-economic pressures and cultural factor (Li et al., 2022). DeepSeek has emerged as an advanced large language model, is increasingly recognised for its potential to serve as a robust clinical decision support system (CDSS) for mental health practitioners. DeepSeek's

24/7 availability and scalable architecture enable it to serve as an accessible first point of contact for individuals who may be reluctant or unable to engage with traditional mental health services. The effectiveness of DeepSeek in this context is supported by its ability to deliver empathetic and contextually relevant responses. For instance, a news report highlighted the experience of a 28-year-old user who engaged with DeepSeek for nightly emotional processing, noting its profound impact: "DeepSeek has been such an amazing counsellor. It has helped me look at things from different perspectives and does a better job than the paid counselling services I have tried" (Kelly, 2025). This user's account underscores DeepSeek's capacity to provide meaningful emotional support, particularly in settings where traditional services are inaccessible. Experimental studies further validate these observations. Mu and Li (2025) compared DeepSeek's performance to ChatGPT using 21 prompts related to depression, anxiety, and substance abuse among Chinese university students, finding that DeepSeek generated more diverse and tailored responses, enhancing its suitability for early intervention.

Despite these strengths in prompt-based responses, DeepSeek's application in more dynamic, real-world scenarios such as simulating full psychological counselling sessions has highlighted certain limitations. In a study exploring role-playing interactions between LLMs to mimic counsellor-client dialogues, Qiu and Lan (2024) tested DeepSeek-V2-Chat (DeepSeek-AI et al., 2024) as both a simulated client and counsellor. The results showed that DeepSeek, unlike GPT-4, struggled to produce human-like interactions, often generating either overly lengthy utterances or abbreviated turns that did not align with realistic counselling dynamics. This indicates that while DeepSeek performs well in static or triage-oriented applications, its use in extended, interactive mental health simulations requires additional fine-tuning to better replicate natural conversational flow and depth in therapeutic settings.

DEEPSEEK'S ROLE AS A CLINICAL DECISION SUPPORT FOR PRACTITIONERS

DeepSeek's ability to rapidly synthesise and contextualise vast amounts of biomedical literature, clinical guidelines, and patient data enables practitioners to make more informed, timely, and personalised decisions in complex clinical scenarios (Temsah et al., 2025). DeepSeek's architecture allows for integration with electronic health records (EHRs) and other digital health systems, facilitating seamless access to patient histories, laboratory results, and progress notes (Li et al., 2024; Zhou et al., 2025). These attributes position DeepSeek as a transformative clinical decision support system, advancing personalised, evidence-based, and equitable healthcare delivery.

Prompt formulation is a pivotal step in DeepSeek's clinical decision support process, as illustrated in Figure 6.1. Both patient-reported and clinician-supplied inputs including symptoms, clinical observations, and relevant demographic data are synthesised with structured information from EHRs to construct comprehensive prompts. This process ensures that the DeepSeek LLM receives a clear, context-rich query, enhancing the accuracy and relevance of its diagnostic reasoning. Effective prompt formulation emphasises clarity, completeness, and contextual detail. For clinicians, this involve standardised templates or medical terminologies, while for general users, prompts are designed to capture key symptoms and concerns. Incorporating chain-of-thought instructions within prompts can further encourage DeepSeek to provide transparent, stepwise explanations, supporting clinical review and trust.

User surveys reveal that both clinicians and patients are receptive to using DeepSeek as a support tool, provided it is easy to use, trustworthy, and integrated with human oversight to mitigate risks associated with bias, data privacy, and hallucinations (Choudhury

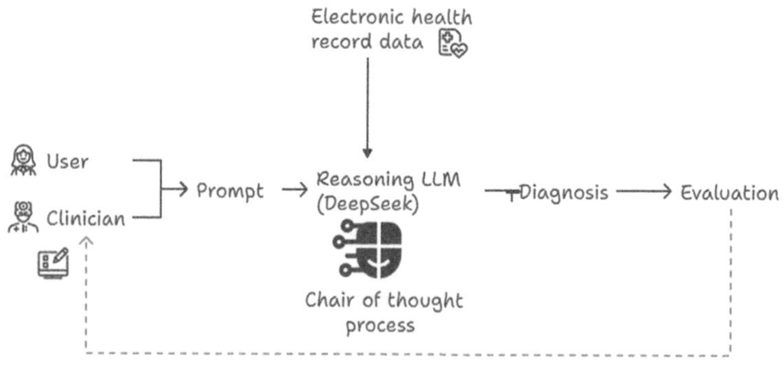

Figure 6.1 Simplified clinical decision support workflow for DeepSeek.

et al., 2025; Temsah et al., 2025). Recent comparative studies showed DeepSeek's strengths in clinical reasoning and decision support, particularly in specialised domains such as mental health, neurology, and oncology (Benchmark evaluation of DeepSeek large language models in clinical decision-making | Nature Medicine, n.d.; Gupta et al., 2025). For example, DeepSeek-R1 has demonstrated outstanding accuracy in mental health diagnosis and knowledge assessment tasks, outperforming both proprietary and open-source LLMs on standardised benchmarks (Gupta et al., 2025; Xu et al., 2025). DeepSeek-R1 achieved disease-level accuracies as high as 100% in mental health scenarios, and its predictive confidence was rated among the highest in the field (Gupta et al., 2025). In experimental studies involving Chinese university students, Mu and Li (2025) compared DeepSeek and ChatGPT using 21 prompts addressing issues such as depression, anxiety, and substance abuse. They found that DeepSeek produced a greater diversity of responses compared to ChatGPT, highlighting its adaptability in educational and clinical mental health contexts. Moreover, DeepSeek generates transparent, stepwise reasoning outputs that enable clinicians to review and validate the logic behind its recommendations, an essential feature for promoting interpretability and clinical trust (Ye et al., 2025; Zhou et al., 2025).

Beyond diagnostics, DeepSeek is increasingly being used for care planning, patient engagement, and clinical education. Studies show that DeepSeek's outputs align closely with international clinical guidelines and can generate actionable care plans across a variety of clinical domains (Analyses of different prescriptions for health using artificial intelligence: A critical approach based on the international guidelines of health institutions | Health Information Science and Systems, n.d.; Zhou et al., 2025). Its open-source nature and transparent reasoning steps facilitate adaptation and customisation for local practice needs, making it especially valuable in resource-limited contexts (Temsah et al., 2025).

DEEPSEEK USER EXPERIENCES: BRIDGING EMOTIONAL SUPPORT AND CLINICAL REALITIES

DeepSeek's emergence as an open-source LLM has been recognised for its adaptability, transparency, and offline deployment, features that not only support user trust but also address key concerns around data privacy and regional customisation (Temsah et al., 2025). For example, a recent multinational survey found that users' trust in DeepSeek is strongly influenced by its perceived ease of use and usefulness, with over half of respondents indicating intentions to adopt DeepSeek for health-related queries over other LLMs (Choudhury et al., 2025). The survey also emphasised that trust mediates users' willingness to rely on the platform, while risk perception remains a significant barrier to adoption.

EMOTIONAL SUPPORT AND MENTAL HEALTH TRIAGE: REAL USER NARRATIVES

DeepSeek's potential in scalable mental health triage becomes most evident when viewed through the lens of real user experiences. Personal narratives illuminate not only the profound emotional connections users form with the system but also the persistent divide between consumer satisfaction and clinical rigor. User testimonials highlight DeepSeek's exceptional capacity for empathetic engagement, particularly among young adults facing mental health stigma and limited care access (Peter et al., 2021). In a BBC report (Kelly, 2025), "Holly" (28, Guangzhou) described nightly "therapy sessions" with DeepSeek following her grandmother's death, noting:

> It helped me look at things from different perspectives and does a better job than paid counselling services I've tried. [...] I've forgotten my own voice and soul—thank you, AI.

Similarly, an anonymous user from Hubei province reported crying when DeepSeek's "thought process" feature revealed its reasoning about her emotional struggles:

> DeepSeek has introduced new perspectives that freed me [...] It tries to understand your question and get to know you as a person.
>
> (Kelly, 2025)

These testimonials are echoed by broader user surveys, which highlight DeepSeek's capacity to foster emotional connection and trust, particularly among young adults facing mental health stigma and limited access to traditional care (Choudhury et al., 2025).

EDUCATIONAL IMPACT: DEEPSEEK IN STEM LEARNING

Beyond mental health, DeepSeek's targeted models have also demonstrated value in STEM education. Recent research shows that DeepSeek-R1, DeepSeek-Math, and DeepSeek-Coder address the limitations of general LLMs by providing structured reasoning, stepwise problem-solving, and adaptive feedback in technical and programming contexts (Neha and Bhati, n.d.). These models enable personalised learning, enhance engagement, and support deeper conceptual understanding, though challenges such as student overreliance and algorithmic bias remain and require responsible integration and robust educator oversight (Huang et al., 2025). Table 6.1 presents qualitative overview of DeepSeek's core model variants, summarising their principal capabilities, application domains, and user experiences.

CHALLENGES IN DEPLOYING DEEPSEEK FOR MENTAL HEALTH

Despite these transformative capabilities, DeepSeek face several critical challenges when deployed in mental health contexts (see Figure 6.2). One major concern is bias and fairness: since DeepSeek learn from large datasets that may contain historical or cultural biases, their outputs can inadvertently perpetuate stereotypes or provide responses that are insensitive to certain groups, potentially undermining equity and inclusivity. Closely related is the issue of clinical appropriateness and safety. While LLMs can generate plausible-sounding advice, they lack the clinical expertise and judgement capability of trained mental health professionals. This limitation can result in responses that are not aligned with best practices or fail to address the complexities of individual cases, posing potential risks to user well-being.

Another challenge is the lack of explainability. LLMs operate as "black boxes," making it difficult for users, clinicians, or regulators to understand the rationale behind specific outputs. This opacity complicates the auditing of AI recommendations and can hinder the building of trust, which is especially critical in sensitive domains such as mental health. Finally, ambiguity and sarcasm in user communication present persistent difficulties for LLMs. These models

Table 6.1 Qualitative overview of DeepSeek model applications

DeepSeek variant	*Core strengths and capabilities*	*Primary application domains*	*Notable user experiences*	*Open-source URL*
DeepSeek-V3	Highly versatile, transparent reasoning; multilingual open-source architecture	Generalist: Mental health triage, cross-disciplinary education	Trusted for empathetic engagement and privacy	• https://github.com/deepseek-ai/DeepSeek-V3
DeepSeek-R1	**Advanced logical structuring**; stepwise problem-solving; evidence-based reasoning	**STEM education**, clinical decision support, research analysis	**Enables deeper conceptual understanding** in complex subjects	• https://github.com/deepseek-ai/DeepSeek-R1
DeepSeek-Math	Step-by-step solutions; **adaptive feedback loops**; error diagnosis	Math education (algebra→calculus), competitive exam prep	**Personalised mastery tracking**; reduces learning anxiety	• https://github.com/deepseek-ai/DeepSeek-Math
DeepSeek-Coder	Context-aware code generation; **real-time debugging**; project-scale optimisation	Computer science education; **developer skill-building**	Accelerates **experiential coding proficiency**	• https://github.com/deepseek-ai/DeepSeek-Coder

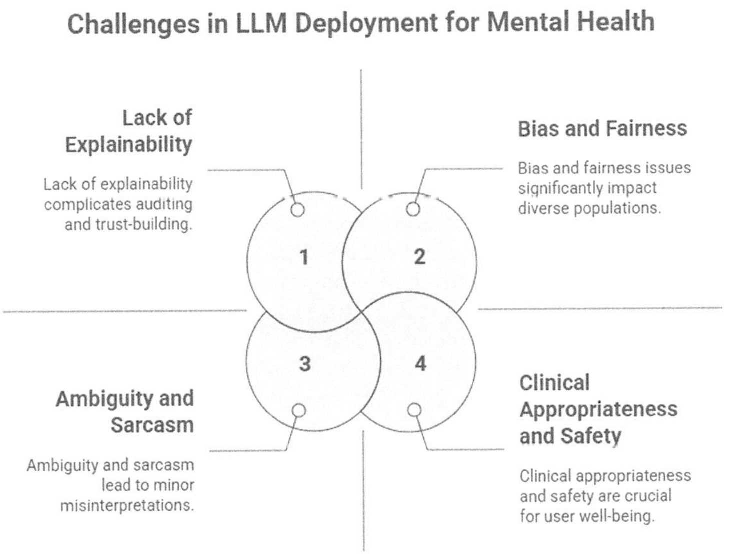

Figure 6.2 Key challenges in LLM deployment for mental health.

may misinterpret jokes, irony, or culturally specific expressions, leading to minor misinterpretations or, in some cases, significant misunderstandings. These challenges highlight the importance of ongoing research and multidisciplinary collaboration to refine LLM deployment in mental health care, ensuring both the safety and fairness of AI driven interventions.

CONCLUSION

DeepSeek represents a transformative step in leveraging large language models for mental health care, offering scalable emotional support and robust clinical decision assistance. Its open-source framework, empathetic engagement, and integration with clinical systems enable it to address critical gaps in mental health access, particularly for underserved populations. However, challenges such as model bias, limited explainability, and the need for culturally sensitive responses highlight the importance of cautious deployment. By addressing these limitations through ongoing research and multidisciplinary collaboration, DeepSeek can pave the way for responsible and equitable AI-driven mental health solutions, balancing innovation with clinical rigor and ethical considerations.

REFERENCES

Babu, A., & Joseph, A. P. (2024). Artificial intelligence in mental healthcare: Transformative potential vs. the necessity of human interaction. *Frontiers in Psychology*, 15. https://doi.org/10.3389/fpsyg.2024.1378904

Choudhury, A., Shahsavar, Y., & Shamszare, H. (2025). User Intent to Use DeepSeek for Health Care Purposes and Their Trust in the Large Language Model: Multinational Survey Study. *JMIR Human Factors*, 12(1), e72867. https://doi.org/10.2196/72867

Campos, V. M. S., Prudente, T. P., Leão, L. L., da Costa, M. S., Oliva, H. N. P., & Monteiro-Junior, R. S. (2025). Analyses of different prescriptions for health using artificial intelligence: A critical approach based on the international guidelines of health institutions. Health Information Science and Systems, 13(1), 52. https://link.springer.com/article/10.1007/s13755-025-00368-0

DeepSeek-AI, Liu, A., Feng, B., Wang, B., Wang, B., Liu, B., Zhao, C., Dengr, C., Ruan, C., Dai, D., Guo, D., Yang, D., Chen, D., Ji, D., Li, E., Lin, F., Luo, F., Hao, G., Chen, G., … Xie, Z. (2024). DeepSeek-V2: A Strong, Economical, and Efficient Mixture-of-Experts Language Model (No. arXiv:2405.04434). arXiv. https://doi.org/10.48550/arXiv.2405.04434

Deng, Z., Ma, W., Han, Q.-L., Zhou, W., Zhu, X., Wen, S., & Xiang, Y. (2025). Exploring DeepSeek: A Survey on Advances, Applications, Challenges and Future Directions. *IEEE/CAA Journal of Automatica Sinica*, 12(5), 872–893. https://doi.org/10.1109/JAS.2025.125498

Gupta, G. K., Pande, P., Acharya, N., Singh, A. K., & Niroula, S. (2025). LLMs in Disease Diagnosis: A Comparative Study of DeepSeek-R1 and O3 Mini Across Chronic Health Conditions (No. arXiv:2503.10486). arXiv. https://doi.org/10.48550/arXiv.2503.10486

Hong, T., & Hu, M. (2025). Opportunities, Challenges, and Regulatory Responses to China's AI Computing Power Development under DeepSeek's Changing Landscape. *International Journal of Digital Law and Governance*, 2(1), 83–105, https://doi.org/10.1515/ijdlg-2025-0002

Huang, L., Yu, W., Ma, W., Zhong, W., Feng, Z., Wang, H., Chen, Q., Peng, W., Feng, X., Qin, B., & Liu, T. (2025). A Survey on Hallucination in Large Language Models: Principles, Taxonomy, Challenges, and Open Questions. *ACM Transactions on Information Systems*, 43(2), 1–55. https://doi.org/10.1145/3703155

Kelly, N.. (2025, February 12). "DeepSeek brought me to tears": How young Chinese find therapy in AI. https://www.bbc.com/news/articles/cy7g45g2nxno

Li, L., Zhou, J., Gao, Z., Hua, W., Fan, L., Yu, H., Hagen, L., Zhang, Y., Assimes, T. L., Hemphill, L., & Ma, S. (2024). A scoping review of using Large Language Models (LLMs) to investigate Electronic Health Records (EHRs) (No. arXiv:2405.03066). arXiv. https://doi.org/10.48550/arXiv.2405.03066

Li, W., Zhao, Z., Chen, D., Peng, Y., & Lu, Z. (2022). Prevalence and associated factors of depression and anxiety symptoms among college students: A systematic review and meta-analysis. *Journal of Child Psychology and Psychiatry*, 63(11), 1222–1230. https://doi.org/10.1111/jcpp.13606

Mu, Y., & Li, Q. (2025). Generative AI for Mental Health Education: A Comparison of ChatGPT and DeepSeek. In X. Meng, L. Wang, H. Chen, H. Chen, S. Xu, & X.-X. Zhan (Eds.), *Big Data and Social Computing* (pp. 411–416). Springer Nature. https://doi.org/10.1007/978-981-95-0880-8_34

Naik, A., Thomas, J., Sree, T., & Reddy, H. (2025). Artificial Empathy: AI based Mental Health (No. arXiv:2506.00081). arXiv. https://doi.org/10.48550/arXiv.2506.00081

Neha, F., & Bhati, D. (2025). DeepSeek Models in STEM Education: Capabilities, Applications, and Challenges. Retrieved September 10, 2025, from https://www.authorea.com/doi/full/10.36227/techrxiv.174198447.71647707?commit=e4d293fd5f0a84707cb0dfb7fa806e9a319bd4b7

Organization (2022). World mental health report: Transforming mental health for all. World Health Organization.

Peter, L.-J., Schindler, S., Sander, C., Schmidt, S., Muehlan, H., McLaren, T., Tomczyk, S., Speerforck, S., & Schomerus, G. (2021). Continuum beliefs and mental illness stigma: A systematic review and meta-analysis of correlation and intervention studies. *Psychological Medicine*, 51(5), 716–726. https://doi.org/10.1017/S0033291721000854

Qiu, H., & Lan, Z. (2024). Interactive Agents: Simulating Counselor-Client Psychological Counseling via Role-Playing LLM-to-LLM Interactions (No. arXiv:2408.15787). arXiv. https://doi.org/10.48550/arXiv.2408.15787

Sallam, M., Al-Mahzoum, K., Sallam, M., & Mijwil, M. M. (2025). DeepSeek: Is it the End of Generative AI Monopoly or the Mark of the Impending Doomsday? *Mesopotamian Journal of Big Data*, 2025, 26–34. https://doi.org/10.58496/MJBD/2025/002

Sandmann, S., Hegselmann, S., Fujarski, M., Bickmann, L., Wild, B., Eils, R., & Varghese, J. (2025). Benchmark evaluation of DeepSeek large language models in clinical decision-making. *Nature Medicine*, 31(8), 2546–2549. https://doi.org/10.1038/s41591-025-03727-2

Sorin, V., Brin, D., Barash, Y., Konen, E., Charney, A., Nadkarni, G., & Klang, E. (2024). Large Language Models and Empathy: Systematic Review. *Journal of Medical Internet Research*, 26(1), e52597. https://doi.org/10.2196/52597

Sandmann, S., Hegselmann, S., & Fujarski, M. (2025). Benchmark evaluation of DeepSeek large language models in clinical decision-making. Nature Medicine, 31(8), 2546–2549. https://www.nature.com/articles/s41591-025-03727-2

Temsah, A., Alhasan, K., Altamimi, I., Jamal, A., Al-Eyadhy, A., Malki, K. H., & Temsah, M.-H. (2025). DeepSeek in Healthcare: Revealing Opportunities and Steering Challenges of a New Open-Source Artificial

Intelligence Frontier. *Cureus*, 17(2), e79221. https://doi.org/10.7759/cureus.79221

Xu, Y., Fang, Z., Lin, W., Jiang, Y., Jin, W., Balaji, P., Wang, J., & Xia, T. (2025). Evaluation of large language models on mental health: From knowledge test to illness diagnosis. *Frontiers in Psychiatry*, 16. https://doi.org/10.3389/fpsyt.2025.1646974

Ye, J., Bronstein, S., Hai, J., & Hashish, M. A. (2025). DeepSeek in Healthcare: A Survey of Capabilities, Risks, and Clinical Applications of Open-Source Large Language Models (No. arXiv:2506.01257). arXiv. https://doi.org/10.48550/arXiv.2506.01257

Zeng, D., Qin, Y., Sheng, B., & Wong, T. Y. (2025). DeepSeek's "Low-Cost" Adoption Across China's Hospital Systems: Too Fast, Too Soon? *Journal of the American Medical Association*, 333(21), 1866–1869. https://doi.org/10.1001/jama.2025.6571

Zhou, J., Cheng, Y., He, S., Chen, Y., & Chen, H. (2025). Large Language Models for Transforming Healthcare: A Perspective on DeepSeek-R1. *MedComm – Future Medicine*, 4(2), e70021. https://doi.org/10.1002/mef2.70021

Part III

Looking forward

Chapter 7

Risks and ethical considerations of using artificial intelligence in mental health care

Olive K. L. Woo

INTRODUCTION

The emergence of DeepSeek—an advanced open-source large language model first appeared in public eye in 2023—that has been used for mental health support highlights the urgent need for robust ethical frameworks. As DeepSeek powers applications ranging from diagnostic support in hospitals to AI-driven mental health chatbots, it presents both opportunities and ethical challenges. This chapter examines the relevant ethical principles and potential risks that demands immediate attention.

ETHICAL PRINCIPLES IN HEALTH CARE

Ethical principles serve as the foundation for responsible decision-making by healthcare practitioners, ensuring patient safety, well-being, and trust. The World Health Organization (2021a) articulates a unified set of ethical principles specifically for AI in health care, including beneficence, nonmaleficence, autonomy, justice, and explicability (Gorelik et al., 2025; Oniani et al., 2023; World Health Organization, 2021b). These principles serve as a helpful framework for the development, deployment, and oversight of AI systems like DeepSeek in mental health care (Saeidnia et al., 2024).

Beneficence

The first ethical principle for AI intervention is *beneficence* (Gorelik et al., 2025; World Health Organization, 2021a). It highlights the importance of enhancing individuals' well-being while protecting their

DOI: 10.1201/9781003649137-10

dignity. In other words, user's well-being should be prioritised at all times. As DeepSeek has been emergently deployed in hospital diagnostics and mental health support that aims to enhance patient outcomes and reduce clinician workload (Chen & Zhang, 2025; Temsah et al., 2025), AI should serve the benefit of the general public and promote the well-being of individuals.

Nonmaleficence

The second principle is *nonmaleficence* (Gorelik et al., 2025; World Health Organization, 2021a). Alongside enhancing the overall well-being of the public, it is crucial to prioritise the prevention of any harm to users. The major proposition of the nonmaleficence principle is doing no harm to users. Despite the benefits, the use of DeepSeek in hospital diagnostics and mental health support involve risks. They include automation bias, hallucinations, and the potential for erroneous recommendations, all of which necessitate rigorous validation and ongoing human oversight to prevent harm (Chen & Zhang, 2025; Temsah et al., 2025).

Autonomy

Another ethical principle is *autonomy*, advocating the importance of individual's ability to make informed decisions and independent decisions (Gorelik et al., 2025; World Health Organization, 2021a). AI should be used to guide individuals in making decisions but not to override their own judgements. An optimal balance should be achieved between the decisions made by the clinician and by the AI system. This prevents a skewed decision process towards AI technology. As such, DeepSeek should function as an assistive tool, ensuring that clinicians and users retain ultimate control over decisions. In mental health contexts, where users may form strong emotional connections with AI chatbots, it is crucial to maintain clear boundaries and informed consent, which serve to protect their rights to privacy and decision-making (Mennella et al., 2024; Tavory, 2024; UK Parliamentary, 2025).

Justice

Justice is another fundamental principle in the application of AI for mental health support (Gorelik et al., 2025; World Health Organization, 2021a). Fairness is essential in healthcare services as it ensures all members of the community can access psychotherapy according to their needs. AI should be appropriately used to promote equity and guard against discriminations towards minority groups. As such, the deployment of DeepSeek should promote equitable access to AI-driven health care, avoiding the reinforcement of existing biases or the exclusion of vulnerable groups. Evaluating DeepSeek for algorithmic fairness and cultural sensitivity is essential, especially in diverse populations (Temsah et al., 2025; UK Parliamentary, 2025).

Explicability

Explicability promotes transparency and accountability of AI-assisted interventions (Gorelik et al., 2025; World Health Organization, 2021a). This is a unique ethical principle specifically applied to AI interventions. Transparency in the application of AI systems depends on clear communication about AI technologies, along with detailed reporting of their evidence base and known limitations (Chustecki, 2024; Gutierrez et al., 2024). DeepSeek's open-source nature and support for local, offline deployment can enhance transparency and data privacy. However, explicability also requires that users and clinicians understand how DeepSeek arrives at its conclusions, and that they can challenge or override AI-generated advice when necessary (Temsah et al., 2025).

ETHICAL CONSIDERATIONS IN MENTAL HEALTHCARE

The previous section discussed the ethical principles for the use of AI in health care. This section proceeds to introduce the critical ethical concerns in mental health context such as data privacy, algorithmic bias, risk of dehumanisation, and accountability.

Data privacy and security

Ensuring the privacy and security of mental health data is critical, particularly when using AI systems in healthcare contexts. Regulatory frameworks like the General Data Protection Regulation (GDPR) in Europe and the Health Insurance Portability and Accountability Act (HIPAA) in the United States establish foundational requirements for safeguarding patient confidentiality, mandating measures such as data encryption, anonymisation, and secure storage to mitigate risks of unauthorised access and data breaches (Pesapane et al., 2021; Torous et al., 2018). The study of Wang et al. (2022) compares operational rules for healthcare data used in AI across China, the United States, and the European Union. Key issues identified include differing concepts of privacy and personal information, the impact of technological advancements on informed consent, and tensions between freedom and security in cross-border data flow regulations. The study highlights the need to balance privacy protections with technological development, individual and group interests, and corporate profits with public interest. The study recommends China, in particular, to enact specific regulations for healthcare data, defining and classifying healthcare information clearly, and implementing stricter accountability measures.

Algorithmic bias and fairness

Algorithmic bias poses a major challenge to ensuring the fair and equitable implementation of AI systems in mental health care. AI models are inherently shaped by the datasets used for their training. If these datasets are unrepresentative or biased, the resulting algorithms may perpetuate or exacerbate disparities in mental healthcare delivery (Timmons et al., 2023; Ueda et al., 2024). Bias in AI systems can manifest in several ways, including differential accuracy rates across demographic groups, culturally insensitive therapeutic recommendations, and the reinforcement of harmful stereotypes. For example, study has shown that AI models in health care frequently exhibit poorer performance for minority populations, largely due to their underrepresentation in training data (Obermeyer et al., 2019). AI-driven therapeutic tools may perpetuate cultural biases, leading to recommendations that are not culturally appropriate or effective (Bender et al., 2021).

To mitigate these risks, it is essential to curate diverse and representative training datasets that reflect the heterogeneity of real-world populations. Research emphasises that incorporating demographic diversity and contextual factors into training data improves model fairness and accuracy (Mehrabi et al., 2021). This requires collaboration between data scientists, clinicians, and social scientists to ensure that the training data accounts for cultural, linguistic, and socioeconomic variations (Char et al., 2020). Techniques such as fairness-aware machine learning, which incorporates fairness constraints into algorithm design and algorithmic transparency measures can further enhance the equity and accountability of AI systems (Obermeyer et al., 2019).

Risk of dehumanisation

A significant concern tied to the integration of AI in mental health care is the potential diminishing of human-centred care. Psychotherapy is fundamentally rooted in the therapeutic alliance—a collaborative, empathetic relationship between the patient and the therapist as a cornerstone of effective treatment (Stubbe, 2018). While AI systems can simulate therapeutic dialogues and provide evidence-based recommendations, they lack the genuine empathy, emotional intelligence, and contextual understanding that human therapists bring to the therapeutic process (Fiske, Henningsen, & Buyx, 2019). Research highlights that AI-driven interventions, though promising in scalability and accessibility, cannot fully replicate the nuanced human connection essential for mental health recovery (Luxton, 2014). Over-reliance on AI risks may reduce complex human experiences to algorithmic outputs, potentially undermining the depth and authenticity of care (Torous & Nebeker, 2017).

Research has also shown that while conversational AI can provide valuable support and education, users often report limitations in the flexibility and naturalness of dialogue, which can lead to feelings of frustration or lack of connection (Laranjo et al., 2018; Meadows et al., 2020). The inability of current AI systems to fully interpret nuanced emotional states or culturally specific expressions can hinder their effectiveness and reduce patient engagement (Bickmore et al., 2010). It also involves risk on overemphasising quantitative data which neglects the qualitative, contextual aspects of mental health (Meadows et al., 2020; Miner et al., 2017).

While AI-enabled tools can enhance accessibility and continuity of care, they require careful design to ensure they complement rather than replace the human elements essential to mental health treatment (Miner et al., 2017; Laranjo et al., 2018). To preserve the humanistic essence of psychotherapy, AI should be positioned as a *complementary* tool rather than a replacement for human therapists. *Hybrid models of care*, where AI systems augment but do not replace human expertise, offer a promising approach to integrating technology while maintaining the integrity of the therapeutic relationship. For instance, AI can assist therapists by providing real-time insights into patient progress, identifying patterns that may inform treatment decisions, or automating administrative tasks to free up therapists' time for direct patient interaction (Fitzpatrick et al., 2017). Such approaches ensure that the therapeutic alliance remains central to the treatment process while using AI to enhance effectiveness.

Accountability and liability

The application of AI in mental health care raises concerns about accountability and liability, particularly in cases where AI-driven interventions result in harmful or adverse outcomes. Unlike traditional therapeutic practices, where responsibility lies solely with the therapist, AI diffuses accountability across multiple stakeholders, including software developers, data scientists, clinicians, and regulatory bodies, complicating legal and ethical standards for malpractice or harm (Cheong, 2024; Floridi et al., 2018). If an AI system provides an inaccurate diagnosis or inappropriate therapeutic recommendation that harms a patient, it is challenging to pinpoint whether the fault lies with the AI model's design, its training data quality, or the clinician's reliance on its output (Habli et al., 2020). Moreover, transparency and algorithmic explainability are critical to ensuring accountability, as opaque "black box" AI models hinder understanding and oversight, increasing risks to patient safety (Cheong, 2024; Floridi et al., 2018).

To address these challenges, comprehensive regulatory frameworks should clearly delineate roles and responsibilities, incorporating independent audits, algorithmic transparency, liability insurance, and dynamic safety assurance models that evolve post-deployment (Habli et al., 2020). Ethical principles, as elaborated in previous section must be integrated with technical principles like explainability, fairness, and auditability to govern responsible use of AI in mental healthcare (Singhal et al., 2024).

CONCLUSIONS

The integration of AI into healthcare systems presents both opportunities and challenges. While DeepSeek's open-source flexibility and powerful AI capabilities can greatly enhance clinical decision-making and mental health support, they also amplify concerns around data privacy, algorithmic bias, risk of dehumanisation, and accountability. Addressing these issues requires a robust ethical framework, vigilant human oversight, and ongoing evaluation to ensure that AI interventions remain transparent, fair, and aligned with the core ethics and values of patient care. At the end, the responsible adoption of DeepSeek hinges on balancing innovation with ethical integrity, ensuring that technological advancement serves to enhance—not compromise—the safety, trust, and well-being of people with psychological needs.

REFERENCES

Bender, E. M., Gebru, T., McMillan-Major, A., & Shmitchell, S. (2021). On the dangers of stochastic parrots: Can language models be too big? In *Proceedings of the 2021 ACM Conference on Fairness, Accountability, and Transparency* (pp. 610–623). https://doi.org/10.1145/3442188.3445922

Bickmore, T., Schulman, D., & Yin, L. (2010). Maintaining engagement in long-term interventions with relational agents. *Applied Artificial Intelligence*, *24*(6), 648–666. https://doi.org/10.1080/08839514.2010.492259

Char, D. S., Shah, N. H., & Magnus, D. (2020). Implementing Machine Learning in Health Care—Addressing Ethical Challenges. *The New England Journal of Medicine*, *378*(11), 981–983. https://doi.org/10.1056/NEJMp1714229

Chen, J., & Zhang, Q. (2025). *DeepSeek reshaping healthcare in China's tertiary hospitals*. https://doi.org/10.48550/arxiv.2502.16732

Cheong, B. C. (2024). Transparency and accountability in AI systems: Safeguarding wellbeing in the age of algorithmic decision-making. *Frontiers in Human Dynamics*, *6*. https://doi.org/10.3389/fhumd.2024.1421273

Chustecki, M. (2024). Benefits and risks of AI in health care: Narrative review. *Interactive Journal of Medical Research*, *13*, e53616. https://doi.org/10.2196/53616

Fiske, A., Henningsen, P., & Buyx, A. (2019). Your robot therapist will see you now: Ethical implications of embodied artificial intelligence in psychiatry, psychology, and psychotherapy. *Journal of Medical Internet Research*, *21*(5), e13216. https://doi.org/10.2196/13216

Fitzpatrick, K. K., Darcy, A., & Vierhile, M. (2017). Delivering cognitive behavioral therapy to young adults with symptoms of depression and anxiety using a fully automated conversational agent (Woebot): A randomized controlled trial. *JMIR Mental Health*, 4(2), e19. https://doi.org/10.2196/mental.7785

Floridi, L. (2023). *The Ethics of Artificial Intelligence: Principles, Challenges, and Opportunities*. Oxford University Press. pp. 243.

Floridi, L., Cowls, J., Beltrametti, M., Chatila, R., Chazerand, P., Dignum, V., ... & Vayena, E. (2018). AI4People—An ethical framework for a good AI society: Opportunities, risks, principles, and recommendations. *Minds and Machines*, *28*(4), 689–707.

Gorelik, A. J., Li, M., Hahne, J., Wang, J., Ren, Y., Yang, L., Zhang, X., Liu, X., Wang, X., Bogdan, R., & Carpenter, B. D. (2025). Ethics of AI in healthcare: a scoping review demonstrating applicability of a foundational framework. *Frontiers in Digital Health*, *7*, 1662642. https://doi.org/10.3389/fdgth.2025.1662642

Gutierrez, G., Stephenson, C., Eadie, J., Asadpour, K., & Alavi, N. (2024). Examining the role of AI technology in online mental healthcare: Opportunities, challenges, and implications, a mixed-methods review. *Frontiers in Psychiatry*, *15*, 1356773–1356773. https://doi.org/10.3389/fpsyt.2024.1356773

Habli, I., Lawton, T., & Porter, Z. (2020). Artificial intelligence in health care: Accountability and safety. *Bulletin of the World Health Organization*, *98*(4), 251–256. https://doi.org/10.2471/BLT.19.237487

Laranjo, L., Dunn, A. G., Tong, H. L., Kocaballi, A. B., Chen, J., Bashir, R., ... & Coiera, E. (2018). Conversational agents in healthcare: A systematic review. *Journal of the American Medical Informatics Association*, *25*(9), 1248–1258. https://doi.org/10.1093/jamia/ocy072

Luxton, D. D. (2014). Recommendations for the ethical use and design of artificial intelligent care providers. *Artificial Intelligence in Medicine*, *62*(1), 1–10. https://doi.org/10.1016/j.artmed.2014.06.004

Meadows, R., Hine, C., & Suddaby, E. (2020). Conversational agents and the making of mental health recovery. *Digital Health*, *6*, 2055207620966170. https://doi.org/10.1177/2055207620966170

Mehrabi, N., Morstatter, F., Saxena, N., Lerman, K., & Galstyan, A. (2021). A Survey on Bias and Fairness in Machine Learning. *ACM Computing Surveys*, *54*(6), 1–35. https://doi.org/10.1145/3457607

Mennella, C., Maniscalco, U., De Pietro, G., & Esposito, M. (2024). Ethical and regulatory challenges of AI technologies in healthcare: A narrative review. *Heliyon*, *10*(4), e26297. https://doi.org/10.1016/j.heliyon.2024.e26297

Miner, A. S., Milstein, A., & Hancock, J. T. (2017). Talking to machines about personal mental health problems. *JAMA: The Journal of the American Medical Association*, *318*(13), 1217–1218. https://doi.org/10.1001/jama.2017.14151

Obermeyer, Z., Powers, B., Vogeli, C., & Mullainathan, S. (2019). Dissecting racial bias in an algorithm used to manage the health of populations. *Science*, *366*(6464), 447–453. https://doi.org/10.1126/science.aax2342

Oniani, D., Hilsman, J., Peng, Y. et al. (2023). Adopting and expanding ethical principles for generative artificial intelligence from military to healthcare. *npj Digital Medicine*, *6*, 225. https://doi.org/10.1038/s41746-023-00965-x

Pesapane, F., Bracchi, D. A., Mulligan, J. F., Linnikov, A., Maslennikov, O., Lanzavecchia, M. B., ... & Carrafiello, G. (2021). Legal and regulatory framework for AI solutions in healthcare in EU, US, China, and Russia: New scenarios after a pandemic. *Radiation*, *1*(4), 261–276.

Saeidnia, H. R., Hashemi Fotami, S. G., Lund, B., & Ghiasi, N. (2024). Ethical considerations in artificial intelligence interventions for mental health and well-being: Ensuring responsible implementation and impact. *Social Sciences (Basel)*, *13*(7), 381.

Singhal, A., Neveditsin, N., Tanveer, H., & Mago, V. (2024). Toward fairness, accountability, transparency, and ethics in AI for social media and health care: Scoping review. *JMIR Medical Informatics*, *12*, e50048. https://doi.org/10.2196/50048

Stubbe D. E. (2018). The therapeutic alliance: The fundamental element of psychotherapy. *Focus (American Psychiatric Publishing)*, *16*(4), 402–403. https://doi.org/10.1176/appi.focus.20180022

Tavory T. (2024). Regulating AI in mental health: Ethics of care perspective. *JMIR Mental Health*, *11*, e58493. https://doi.org/10.2196/58493

Temsah, A., Alhasan, K., Altamimi, I., Jamal, A., Al-Eyadhy, A., Malki, K. H., & Temsah, M. H. (2025). DeepSeek in healthcare: Revealing opportunities and steering challenges of a new open-source artificial intelligence frontier. *Cureus*, *17*(2), e79221. https://doi.org/10.7759/cureus.79221

Timmons, A. C., Duong, J. B., Simo Fiallo, N., Lee, T., Vo, H. P. Q., Ahle, M. W., Comer, J. S., Brewer, L. C., Frazier, S. L., & Chaspari, T. (2023). A call to action on assessing and mitigating bias in artificial Intelligence applications for mental health. *Perspectives on Psychological Science: A Journal of the Association for Psychological Science*, *18*(5), 1062–1096. https://doi.org/10.1177/17456916221134490

Torous, J., & Nebeker, C. (2017). Navigating ethics in the digital age: Introducing connected and open research ethics (CORE), a tool for researchers and institutional review boards. *Journal of Medical Internet Research*, *19*(2), e38–e38. https://doi.org/10.2196/jmir.6793

Torous, J., Rodriguez-Villa, E., Brenner, C., & Goulding, J. (2018). Clinical review of user engagement with mental health smartphone apps: Evidence, theory, and improvements. *Evidence-Based Mental Health*, *21*(4), 116–119.

Ueda, D., Kakinuma, T., Fujita, S., Kamagata, K., Fushimi, Y., Ito, R., Matsui, Y., Nozaki, T., Nakaura, T., Fujima, N., Tatsugami, F., Yanagawa, M., Hirata, K., Yamada, A., Tsuboyama, T., Kawamura, M., Fujioka, T., & Naganawa, S. (2024). Fairness of artificial intelligence in healthcare: Review and recommendations. *Japanese Journal of Radiology*, *42*(1), 3–15. https://doi.org/10.1007/s11604-023-01474-3

UK Parliamentary (2025). *AI and mental healthcare: Ethical and regulatory considerations* (POSTnote No. 738). UK Parliament. https://researchbriefings.files.parliament.uk/documents/POST-PN-0738/POST-PN-0738.pdf

Wang, C., Zhang, J., Lassi, N., & Zhang, X. (2022). Privacy protection in using artificial intelligence for healthcare: Chinese regulation in comparative perspective. *Healthcare (Basel, Switzerland)*, *10*(10), 1878. https://doi.org/10.3390/healthcare10101878

World Health Organization. (2021a). *Ethics and Governance of Artificial Intelligence for Health*. World Health Organization. https://www.who.int/publications/i/item/9789240029200

World Health Organization. (2021b). *WHO Issues First Global Report on Artificial Intelligence (AI) in Health and Six Guiding Principles for Its Design and Use*. World Health Organization. https://www.who.int/news/item/28-06-2021-who.issues-first-global-report-on-ai-in-health-and-six-guiding-principles-for-its-design-and-use

Chapter 8

Policy implications and regulations of using artificial intelligence in mental health care

Olive K. L. Woo

INTRODUCTION

Throughout this book, we have explored the potential of AI technologies in providing mental health support. As these technologies become increasingly integrated into mental health practices, the need for robust policies and regulations to ensure their safe, ethical, and effective use is paramount. This chapter examines the current regulatory landscape for AI in health care, identifies key challenges in its implementation, and proposes ethical recommendations to guide the responsible adoption of these technologies.

REGULATORY LANDSCAPE IN HEALTH CARE

In recent years, China has implemented several key regulations to govern the use of AI in health care (Schuerger et al., 2024). The *Cybersecurity Law* (网络安全法) serves to safeguard network security and personal data through multi-tiered protection systems and data localisation requirements (中央人民政府, 2021a). The *Data Security Law* (国数据安全法) prioritises the classification and management of sensitive information through a tiered framework, organised based on its potential impact on national security and public interests (中央人民政府, 2021b; Rogier, 2022). The *Personal Information Protection Law* (PIPL) (个人信息保护法) processes sensitive personal data, which requires explicit consent and purpose limitation (中央网络安全和信息化委员会办公室, 2021). Recent studies have highlighted the role of these regulations in addressing privacy risks in AI-driven healthcare systems. For example, research

DOI: 10.1201/9781003649137-11

emphasises the PIPL's limitations in clarifying "separate consent" requirements and cross-border data transfers (Yao & Yang, 2023), which remain critical challenges for AI applications.

In terms of regulatory authority, the National Medical Products Administration (NMPA) (国家药品监督管理局, https://www.nmpa.gov.cn) is responsible for overseeing the safety, efficacy, and quality of medical products on digital health. For instance, the NMPA has developed guiding principles for the registration review of AI medical devices (CIRS, 2022), such as the NMPA's 2022 guidelines for AI-enabled medical software mandate lifecycle management and safety protocols (Han et al., 2024; Ho, 2024). These frameworks are further supported by evolving standards under the *Network Security Law* (网络安全法) and *Data Security Law* (数据安全法), which establish comprehensive guidelines to safeguard cybersecurity and data privacy. (中央网络安全和信息化委员会办公室, 2016; 全国人民代表大会., 2021). As of July 2023, the study of Liu et al. (2024) identifies 59 AI medical devices approved in China through the governmental database. Internationally, the General Data Protection Regulation (GDPR) in Europe sets strict requirements for data handling and user consent for data processing, while the Health Insurance Portability and Accountability Act (HIPAA) safeguards health information within the U.S. healthcare system (Char et al., 2018 Pesapane et al., 2021).

KEY CHALLENGES IN IMPLEMENTATIONS

One major challenge in regulating AI is accountability, as it remains unclear who is responsible for decisions made by AI systems (Schur et al. (2025)). The rapid pace of AI development often outstrips the evolution of legal frameworks, which may result in fragmented and sometimes inconsistent regulations across healthcare systems. Another challenge faced by the traditional healthcare system is the implementation of AI services. The integration of AI technology has to consider factors such as the availability of valid real-world databases for feeding AI algorithms (Koutsouleris et al., 2022), andlimited resources and infrastructure (Stefl & Prosperi, 1985). Ideally, there should be adequate training for the professional and ethical use of AI in health care. Healthcare providers must carefully address the ethical implications of their use (Coeckelbergh, 2019; Li et al., 2022). They should always apply clinical judgement to ensure that patient information remains confidential and to provide accurate diagnoses (Alonso & Siracuse, 2023; Omar, 2020). However, shortage of well-trained mental health professionals in AI interventions remains a challenge across the globe.

RECOMMENDATIONS

Developing comprehensive regulatory frameworks for AI in mental health is crucial to addressing the challenges posed by AI technology. A comparative study by Wang et al. (2022) highlights the need for China to address significant gaps in healthcare-specific AI governance, such as establishing clearer definitions for health information categories and implementing stricter accountability mechanisms for algorithmic predictions in. International collaboration should build on China's leadership in initiatives like the UN's AI capacity-building resolution (co-sponsored by 143 nations) and the Global AI Governance Initiative (Permanent Mission of the People's Republic of China to the UN, 2024; Xinhua, 2024). These initiative helps align international standard while China balances innovation with security (Zhu, 2024; Zou & Zhang, 2025). It agrees with academic recommendations for balancing privacy protections with technological advancement in sensitive health domains (Wang et al., 2022).

Ensuring transparency and accountability in AI tools is essential for responsible application, especially in the mental health field, where algorithmic bias and data security risks require urgent attention. For instance, routine audits of AI algorithms should be carried out regularly to ensure they function as intended and remain free from biasCruz-Gonzalez et al., 2025. These audits align with China's 2021 AI Ethics Risk Prevention Guidelines (网络安全标准实践指南—人工智能伦理安全风险防范指引) (TC260-PG-20211A), which mandates ethical safety risk analyses before AI deployment (National Information Security Standardization Technical Committee, 2021). In cases of AI-related harm, establishing clear guidelines for liability is crucial. Study has emphasised the need for stronger accountability mechanisms in healthcare AI systems, especially given the fragmented governance currently in place (Wang et al., 2022). There is also a necessity for human-AI collaboration frameworks where mental health professionals retain oversight to ensure that algorithmic decisions remain explainable and subject to clinical judgement–a critical safeguard against automated diagnostic errors (Thakkar et al., 2024).

Furthermore, it is essential to ensure data security and privacy, particularly under China's Personal Information Protection Law and Data Security Law. Strong encryption methods, such as partitioned key systems and anonymisation protocols have been found effective in sharing psychiatric data to protect mental health records against unauthorised access (Shi, 2024; Thilakanathan et al., 2016; Zhang et al., 2025). It is also critical to restrict data access to authorised personnel. Regular staff training on data protection protocols should be systematically implemented to address vulnerabilities in big data management (Arain et al., 2019; Shi, 2024). New and ongoing collaboration such as between institutions like Peking University's mental health research centres (Yang, 2024) and hospitals implementing multimodal diagnostic tools (Li et al., 2024) can accelerate innovation while adhering to PIPL requirements.

CONCLUSIONS

This chapter has explored the current regulatory landscape, identified key challenges in implementing AI solutions, and proposed recommendations to address these issues. Robust policies are essential to ensure the safe, ethical, and equitable use of AI in mental health care, safeguarding patient privacy, promoting fairness, and mitigating risks. We call upon policymakers, mental health professionals, and global stakeholders to collaborate in developing a comprehensive regulatory framework that prioritises user safety and ethical practices.

REFERENCES

Alonso, A., & Siracuse, J. J. (2023, September). Protecting patient safety and privacy in the era of artificial intelligence. In *Seminars in Vascular Surgery* (Vol. 36, No. 3, pp. 426–429). WB Saunders.

Arain, M. A., Tarraf, R., Ahmad, A. (2019) Assessing staff awareness and effectiveness of educational training on IT security and privacy in a large healthcare organization. *Journal of Multidisciplinary Healthcare*, *12*:73–81. https://doi.org/10.2147/JMDH.S183275

Char, D. S., Shah, N. H., & Magnus, D. (2018). Implementing machine learning in health care—Addressing ethical challenges. *New England Journal of Medicine*, *378*(11), 981–983.

Chen, N. (2022). Stakeholder power analysis of the facilitators and barriers for telehealth solution implementation in China: A qualitative study of individual users in Beijing and interviews with institutional stakeholders. *JMIR Formative Research*, *6*(1), e19448.

CIRS. (2022). 国家药监局器审中心关于发布人工智能医疗器械注册审查指导原则的通告(2022年第8号). Retrieved from https://www.cirs-group.com/cn/md/gjyjjqszxgyfbrgznylqxzcsczdyzdtg-2022nd8h

Coeckelbergh, M. (2019). Artificial intelligence: Some ethical issues and regulatory challenges. *Technology and Regulation*, *2019*, 31–34.

Cruz-Gonzalez, P., He, A. W.-J., Lam, E. P., Ng, I. M. C., Li, M. W., Hou, R., … Sánchez Vidaña, D. I. (2025). Artificial intelligence in mental health care: A systematic review of diagnosis, monitoring, and intervention applications. *Psychological Medicine*, *55*, e18. https://doi.org/10.1017/S0033291724003295

Ding, J. (2018). Deciphering China's AI dream: The context and implications of China's AI strategy. Retrieved from https://cdn.governance.ai/Deciphering_Chinas_AI-Dream.pdf

Han, Y., Ceross, A., & Bergmann, J. (2024). Regulatory frameworks for AI-enabled medical device software in China: Comparative analysis and review of implications for global manufacturer. *Journal of Medical Internet Research AI*, *3*, e46871. https://doi.org/10.2196/46871

Ho, C. W. L. (2024). "20: Convergence in the regulation of artificial intelligence software as medical device in the Guangdong–Hong Kong–Macao Greater Bay Area of China." In *Research Handbook on Health, AI and the Law*. Cheltenham, UK: Edward Elgar Publishing. Retrieved Apr 28, 2025, from https://doi.org/10.4337/9781802205657.ch20

Ji, M., Chen, X., Genchev, G. Z., Wei, M., & Yu, G. (2021). Status of AI-enabled clinical decision support systems implementations in China. *Methods of Information in Medicine*, *60*(05/06), 123–132.

Jiang, J, & Zheng, Z. (2024). Medical information protection in internet hospital apps in China: Scale development and content analysis. *JMIR mHealth and uHealth*, *12*, e55061.

Katterbauer, K., & Cleenewerck, L. (2024). Artificial intelligence and its impact on healthcare financing in China – A legal analysis. *Financial Law Review*, *2024*, 62–81. https://doi.org/10.4467/22996834FLR.24.004.19816

Koutsouleris, N., Hauser, T. U., Skvortsova, V., & De Choudhury, M. (2022). From promise to practice: Towards the realisation of AI-informed mental health care. *The Lancet Digital Health*, *4*(11), e829–e840.

Li, F., Ruijs, N., & Lu, Y. (2022). Ethics & AI: A systematic review on ethical concerns and related strategies for designing with AI in healthcare. *Ai*, *4*(1), 28–53.

Li, M., Xiong, X., & Xu, B. (2024). Attitudes and perceptions of Chinese oncologists towards artificial intelligence in healthcare: A cross-sectional survey. *Frontiers in Digital Health*, 6, 1371302.

Liu, Y., Yu, W., & Dillon, T. (2024). Regulatory responses and approval status of artificial intelligence medical devices with a focus on China. *npj Digital Medicine*, 7(1), 255.

Marber, P., & Araya, D. (2023). A new generation artificial intelligence development plan. In *Augmented Education in the Global Age* (1st ed., Vol. 1, pp. 221–233). Routledge.

National Information Security Standardization Technical Committee. (2021). *Network Security Standard Practice Guide – Artificial Intelligence Ethics Security Risk Prevention Guidelines (TC260-PG-20211A) (2021 AI Ethics Risk Prevention Guidelines)*. Retrieved from https://nic.swu.edu.cn/__local/3/59/5F/217191E34DDD03236E0CA22CEF3_75DC735A_6C8E5.pdf?e=.pdf

Omar, R. A. (2020). AI, predictive models and medical records: A dangerous decision for healthcare privacy and restoring the sacred trust of patient confidentiality. *Quinnipiac Health LJ*, *24*, 459.

Permanent Mission of the People's Republic of China to the UN. (2024, December 5). *Group of Friends for international cooperation on AI capacity-building formally established.* Permanent Mission of the People's Republic of China to the UN. http://un.china-mission.gov.cn/eng/czthd/202412/t20241220_11508534.htm

Pesapane, F., Bracchi, D. A., Mulligan, J. F., Linnikov, A., Maslennikov, O., Lanzavecchia, M. B., … & Carrafiello, G. (2021). Legal and regulatory framework for AI solutions in healthcare in EU, US, China, and Russia: New scenarios after a pandemic. *Radiation*, *1*(4), 261–276.

Rogier, C. (2022). China's emerging data protection framework. *Journal of Cybersecurity*, *8*(1), tyac011. https://doi.org/10.1093/cybsec/tyac011

Schuerger, C., Venkatram, V., & Quinn, K. (2024). *China and Medical AI*. Center for Security and Emerging Technology.

Schur, E., Brouns, A., Lee, P. (2025) Ethical Analysis of the Responsibility Gap in Artificial Intelligence. *International Journal of Ethics in Social Sciences* 2025;6(4), 1–10. https://ijethics.com/article-1-356-en.html

Shi X. (2024). Reducing privacy risks of China's healthcare big data through the policy framework. *Frontiers in Public Health*, *12*, 1414076.

Stefl, M. E., & Prosperi, D. C. (1985). Barriers to mental health service utilization. *Community Mental Health Journal*, *21*, 167–178.

Thakkar, A., Gupta, A., & De Sousa, A. (2024). Artificial intelligence in positive mental health: A narrative review. *Frontiers in Digital Health*, 6, 1280235.

Thilakanathan, D., Calvo, R. A., Chen, S., Nepal, S., & Glozier, N. (2016). Facilitating secure sharing of personal health data in the cloud. *JMIR Medical Informatics*, *4*(2), e15. https://doi.org/10.2196/medinform.4756

Wang, C., Zhang, J., Lassi, N., & Zhang, X. (2022). Privacy protection in using artificial intelligence for healthcare: Chinese regulation in comparative perspective. *Healthcare (Basel, Switzerland)*, *10*(10), 1878. https://doi.org/10.3390/healthcare10101878

Xinhua. (2024, July 2). *China leads global AI cooperation as 140 nations co-sponsor UN resolution*. Xinhua News. https://english.news.cn/20240702/5ccf6bb8060a4979a18cd5ddeb9c2a5c/c.html

Yang, V. (2024, May 29). JD Health launches AI-driven mental health services. *JD Corporate Blog*. Retrieved from https://jdcorporateblog.com/jd-health-launches-ai-driven-mental-health-services

Yao, Y., & Yang, F. (2023). Overcoming personal information protection challenges involving real-world data to support public health efforts in China. *Frontiers in Public Health*, *11*, 1265050.

Zeng, Y., Lu, E., & Huangfu, C. (2018). *Linking Artificial Intelligence Principles*. https://doi.org/10.48550/arxiv.1812.04814

Zhang, Y., Fan, S., Hui, H., Zhang, N., Li, J., Liao, L., Ke, C., Zhang, D., Su, S., Song, Z., Zhang, Y., Du, Q., Liu, L., Wang, L., Yang, L., Li, J., Xu, L., Xiao, S., Shi, L., Xiao, X., … Behavioral Epidemiology Education Working Commission of CMEA (2025). Privacy protection for open sharing of psychiatric and behavioral research data: Ethical considerations and recommendations. *Alpha Psychiatry*, *26*(1), 38759.

Zhongming, Z., Linong, L., Xiaona, Y., Wangqiang, Z., & Wei, L. (2017). Ministry of Industry and Information Technology of China [ZQ092012B003].

Zhu, J. (2024). *China's Approach to AI Standardisation: State-guided but Enterprise-led*. Finnish Institute of International Affairs (FIIA). https://fiia.fi/en/publication/chinas-approach-to-ai-standardisation

Zou, M., & Zhang, L. (2025). Navigating China's regulatory approach to generative artificial intelligence and large language models. *Cambridge Forum on AI: Law and Governance*, *1*, e8. https://doi.org/10.1017/cfl.2024.4

中央人民政府. (2021a). 中华人民共和国网络安全法. 取自https://www.cac.gov.cn/2016-11/07/c_1119867116.htm

中央人民政府. (2021b). 中华人民共和国数据安全法. 取自http://www.npc.gov.cn/npc/c2/c30834/202106/t20210610_311888.html

新华社 (2017年7月21日). 国务院印发《新一代人工智能发展规划》. 中国政府网. 取自.

中央网络安全和信息化委员会办公室. (2021, August 20). 中华人民共和国个人信息保护法 [Personal Information Protection Law of the People's Republic of China]. China National People's Congress Network. https://www.cac.gov.cn/2021-08/20/c_1631050028355286.htm

中央网络安全和信息化委员会办公室. (2016, November 7). 中华人民共和国网络安全法 [Cybersecurity Law of the People's Republic of China]. Xinhua News Agency. https://www.cac.gov.cn/2016-11/07/c_1119867116.htm

全国人民代表大会. (2021, June 10). 中华人民共和国数据安全法 [*Data Security Law of the People's Republic of China*]. National People's Congress of China. http://www.npc.gov.cn/npc/c2/c30834/202106/t20210610_311888.html

Chapter 9

The future of artificial intelligence in mental health care

Olive K. L. Woo

INTRODUCTION

As mental health challenges continue to rise worldwide, it is essential to anticipate and prepare for the next wave of AI innovations to ensure equitable, ethical, and effective solutions for diverse populations. This chapter takes a global perspective on the future of AI in mental health support, covering key areas such as its potential for addressing global mental health challenges, possible directions of technological advancements, and the importance of interdisciplinary collaboration in shaping the future of AI-driven mental health systems.

POTENTIAL OF ARTIFICIAL INTELLIGENCE

Addressing global mental health challenges

The global mental health crisis presents a formidable challenge, with nearly one billion people affected worldwide and mental disorders accounting for approximately 16% of the global disease burden (Arias et al., 2022). Conditions such as depression and anxiety not only cause immense personal suffering but also impose a staggering economic cost, estimated at around 1 trillion USD annually in lost productivity (Olawade et al., 2024). Traditional mental healthcare systems are often overwhelmed, under-resourced, and geographically uneven, leaving vast populations without adequate access to support (Yong et al., 2025). Another pressing global challenges is the shortage and uneven distribution of mental health professionals. The ratio of psychiatrists per 100,000 people varies dramatically by region, with some areas having fewer than 0.5 psychiatrists per 100,000, severely limiting access to care (Yong et al., 2025). AI technologies offer

DOI: 10.1201/9781003649137-12

possible solutions to address this current and future challenges by virtue of their availability, accessibility, and affordability (See Chapter 3).

Bridging gaps in underserved regions

AI-powered platforms, such as DeepSeek, chatbots and mobile applications can provide scalable, cost-effective alternatives that can reach underserved and remote populations. These tools offer flexible, on-demand mental health support which can help reduce barriers related to cost, stigma, and geographic isolation (Thakkar et al., 2024; Yong et al., 2025). For example, AI chatbots have demonstrated effectiveness in delivering therapeutic interventions and emotional support, expanding mental healthcare accessibility beyond traditional clinical settings. However, populations in rural or low-income areas often lack reliable internet access, digital literacy, and the necessary technological infrastructure to benefit fully from AI-driven interventions Maita et al., (2024). To realise AI's potential globally, investments in infrastructure, education, and culturally sensitive AI design are essential.

Culturally adaptive solutions

AI's effectiveness in mental health care critically depends on its ability to respect and incorporate cultural differences. Mental health expressions, help-seeking behaviours, and treatment preferences vary widely across cultural contexts. DeepSeek is one example as an emerging large language model-based platform that has been studied for its user acceptance and trustworthiness across diverse populations (Choudhury et al., 2025). It has been shown to be easy to use, useful, and trustworthy among users, highlighting its potential as an accessible and culturally sensitive AI tool. Another example is the AI chatbot developed by the Chinese University of Hong Kong, which integrates generative AI into the existing Jockey Club TourHeart + project to provide culturally relevant mental health support to Hong Kong's youth (Erudera News, 2024). Simultaneously, ongoing research projects are exploring culturally sensitive communication styles in AI chatbots for Latino and Chinese populations to optimise user acceptance and clinical outcomes (University of Washington, 2024).

Reducing stigma and increasing accessibility

As mentioned in Part I, Chinese youth population encounter stigma concerning mental health support. AI technologies can play a pivotal role in reducing such stigma by providing anonymous, non-judgemental, and easily accessible support. AI-driven platforms, such as chatbots and mobile apps, offer confidential environments where users can explore mental health resources without fear of discrimination or exposure (Batool et al., 2025; Siddals et al., 2024). Research also shows that human-AI cooperative interactions can foster empathy and reduce stigma towards individuals with mental illness by creating positive social contact experiences through conversational agents (Song et al., 2025). A mixed-methods study conducted by Sehgal et al. (2025) among Indian adolescents reveals that youth prefer text-based, anonymous digital mental health tools offering emotional support and localised content.

TECHNOLOGICAL ADVANCEMENTS FOR MENTAL HEALTH CARE

AI-assisted tools, such as those for assessments, chatbots, wearable devices, virtual reality, and ecological momentary assessment, show great potential in addressing global mental health challenges. This section explores the future research and advancements that aim to to fully realise their potential and ensure ethical adoptions.

AI-assisted assessment

AI systems can support mental health assessments by analysing complex datasets, such as linguistic patterns, facial expressions, and physiological signals, to identify psychological conditions (Cummins et al., 2015; Reece et al., 2017; Shatte et al., 2019). However, challenges such as algorithmic bias remain a significant concern. Future research must prioritise methods to assess and mitigate such biases to ensure equitable outcomes for diverse populations (Timmons et al., 2023). Interdisciplinary collaboration among mental health professionals, data scientists, and ethicists is essential to develop fair-aware AI systems (Kiss et al., 2023 Luxton, 2016). Furthermore, rigorous validation studies are needed to establish the reliability and accuracy of AI-assisted assessments in clinical settings (Graham et al., 2019).

AI-assisted chatbots and virtual therapists

AI-powered chatbots and virtual therapists are groundbreaking innovation in mental health care. These tools appear to bridge the gap in mental health service delivery by offering accessible and cost-effective support. However, current chatbot functionalities remain limited, often resembling the generic guidance found in self-help books rather than providing comprehensive therapeutic interventions (Denecke et al., 2021). Future advancements are likely to enhance chatbot capabilities, incorporating diverse clinical approaches and more personalised interactions, as suggested by recent research on AI integration in mental health care (Fitzpatrick et al., 2017; Inkster et al., 2018). Longitudinal and validation studies are necessary to determine their effectiveness and identify best practices for integration into mental health care, as emphasised in systematic review highlighting the current evidence gaps and the need for rigorous clinical evaluation (Hollis et al., 2017; Miner et al., 2017).

AI-assisted wearable devices and sensors

The integration of AI with wearable devices and sensors has opened new avenues for real-time monitoring of mental health. Advances in wearable technology, driven by miniaturisation and improved functionality, have transformed experimental devices into everyday tools, such as smart rings and fitness trackers (Kim et al., 2022). Devices like the Oura ring and Samsung Galaxy Ring demonstrate the potential for continuous monitoring of stress and emotional states, offering low-cost, long-term solutions for tracking mental health (Nath & Thapliyal, 2021). Consumer interest in using wearables to monitor stress highlights the growing demand for these technologies. However, further research is needed to refine their algorithms and ensure accuracy in detecting subtle emotional and behavioural changes.

AI-assisted virtual reality therapy

Virtual reality (VR) therapy, combined with AI, represents a cutting-edge approach to mental health treatment. AI-assisted VR platforms have been developed to create personalised, immersive therapeutic experiences that adapt to individual needs in real time. These advancements offer potential for treating conditions such as anxiety,

PTSD, and phobias (Freeman et al., 2017). However, the ethical use of AI-driven technologies requires robust regulatory frameworks to protect patient safety and ensure efficacy (Pham 2025). Future research must focus on refining algorithms, assessing both immediate and long-term outcomes, and training healthcare professionals in the use of these tools (Halbig et al., 2022; Iqbal et al., 2024).

AI-assisted ecological momentary assessment

Ecological momentary assessment (EMA) and ecological momentary interventions (EMI) are gaining traction as AI-powered tools for real-time monitoring and intervention in mental health care. Machine learning models help analyse sensitive, real-time data on behavioural, emotional, and physiological changes, providing insights into an individual's mental state. However, these models present challenges, including privacy concerns, bias, and the "black box" problem, where the decision-making process remains opaque (Hassija et al., 2024). Ethical concerns also arise regarding the potential for inappropriate or harmful feedback from adaptive interventions (Yim et al., 2020). To address these issues, explicit regulations and further research are needed to ensure the safety, fairness, and transparency of EMA/EMI systems.

THE ROLE OF COLLABORATION IN SHAPING THE FUTURE

The future of AI in mental health care hinges on robust collaboration among diverse stakeholders, including users, technologists, mental health professionals, policymakers, and international partners. Such collaborations are essential to develop effective, ethical, and culturally sensitive AI tools that can truly enhance mental health outcomes.

Users and communities

Involving users and communities in AI development and implementation is paramount to ensure that technologies meet real-world needs and respect user preferences. Patient and public involvement in AI-assisted mental health care promotes transparency, trust, and ethical accountability (Banerjee et al., 2022; Tavory, 2024; Zidaru et al., 2021). Research highlights the importance of participatory design processes that engage diverse social groups, including individuals with lived experience of mental illness, in every stage from concept to evaluation (Zidaru et al., 2021). Such engagement helps identify ethical concerns, safety issues, and cultural considerations that might otherwise be overlooked.

Technologists and mental health professionals

Collaboration between AI developers and mental health professionals is critical to creating AI tools that are both clinically effective and ethically sound. Mental health experts provide essential domain knowledge that guides the development, validation, and refinement of AI algorithms, ensuring they align with best clinical practices and user needs. For example, integrating AI into mobile applications has enabled functionalities such as medication reminders, mood tracking, and early identification of behavioural changes indicative of mental health conditions like depression (Thakkar et al., 2024). The authors highlight that these tools are most effective when mental health professionals maintain oversight, interpret AI-generated insights, and customise interventions to individual users. The development process should be collaborative involving psychologists, clinicians, and counsellors who help validate AI tools through clinical trials and real-world testing (Ni & Jia, 2025; Tulk Jesso et al., 2022).

Policymakers and regulators

Policymakers play a crucial role in establishing regulations that support innovation, safeguard ethical standards, and ensure patient safety. The rapid evolution of AI technologies demands flexible yet robust governance frameworks that address privacy, bias, accountability, and transparency. For instance, the European Union's Artificial Intelligence Act (2024) employs a risk-based approach to regulate AI systems, including those used in mental health, ensuring appropriate oversight depending on the potential impact of the technology. In the UK, government initiatives such as the NHS AI Lab and funding programmes have accelerated AI adoption in healthcare, including mental health services, while accompanying guidelines support safe procurement and deployment (UK Parliamentary, 2025). Multi-agency advisory bodies and ethics committees are increasingly recommended to oversee AI development, incorporating an *ethics of care* perspective that emphasises relational and emotional dimensions of mental health treatment (Tavory, 2024; UK Parliamentary, 2025).

Global collaborations

Mental health challenges are global in scale, requiring international cooperation to share knowledge, resources, and best practices for AI integration. One notable example is the European Artificial Intelligence Act (AI Act, https://artificialintelligenceact.eu) enacted by the European Union, creating the world's first comprehensive regulatory framework specifically for AI systems across member states and influencing global standards for AI governance (European Commission, 2024). The OECD Principles on Artificial Intelligence (https://oecd.ai/en/ai-principles) is another example that provides a blueprint for innovative, trustworthy, and rights-based AI and have been embraced by 47 adherents, including the EU, G20, and many non-OECD countries (Organisation for Economic Co-operation and Development, 2024). These collaborations are essential for the development of AI solutions that are adaptable to varied cultural contexts and healthcare systems (Thakkar et al., 2024; UK Parliamentary, 2025).

CONCLUSIONS

AI potentiates mental health support; however, there remains ethical challenges. A future where AI creates a more accessible, inclusive, and impactful mental healthcare system depends on integrating AI with therapist oversight, adhering to ethical standards, and fostering global efforts to bridge disparities in care. To realise this vision, continued innovation, interdisciplinary collaboration, and a strong commitment to equity and ethics are essential.

REFERENCES

Arias, D., Saxena, S., & Verguet, S. (2022). Quantifying the global burden of mental disorders and their economic value. *EClinicalMedicine*, 54, 101675. https://doi.org/10.1016/j.eclinm.2022.101675

Artificial Intelligence Act (2024). The AI Act. Official Journal of the European Union on 12 July 2024. https://artificialintelligenceact.eu/the-act

Babu, A., & Joseph, A. P. (2024). Artificial intelligence in mental healthcare: Transformative potential vs. the necessity of human interaction. *Frontiers in Psychology*, *15*, 1378904. https://doi.org/10.3389/fpsyg.2024.1378904

Banerjee, S., Alsop, P., Jones, L., & Cardinal, R. (2022). Patient and public involvement to build trust in artificial intelligence: A framework, tools, and case studies. https://doi.org/10.17863/CAM.82916

Batool, S., Fazal, A., Sajid, U., & Alam, R.s (2025). AI-driven mental health tools: Their potential in reducing stigma in Pakistan. https://www.academia.edu/127134989/AI_Driven_Mental_Health_Tools_Their_Potential_in_Reducing_Stigma_in_Pakistan

Choudhury, A., Shahsavar, Y., & Shamszare, H. (2025). User intent to use DeepSeek for health care purposes and their trust in the large language model: Multinational survey study. *JMIR Human Factors*, *12*, e72867. https://doi.org/10.2196/72867

Cummins, N., Scherer, S., Krajewski, J., Schnieder, S., Epps, J., & Quatieri, T. F. (2015). A review of depression and suicide risk assessment using speech analysis. *Speech Communication*, *71*, 10–49. https://doi.org/10.1016/j.specom.2015.03.004

Denecke, K., Abd-Alrazaq, A., & Househ, M. (2021). Artificial intelligence for chatbots in mental health: Opportunities and challenges. In *Multiple Perspectives on Artificial Intelligence in Healthcare* (pp. 115–128). Springer International Publishing. https://doi.org/10.1007/978-3-030-67303-1_10

Erudera News. (2024). Chinese University of Hong Kong launches AI chatbot to support student mental health. Erudera. https://erudera.com/news/chinese-university-of-hong-kong-launches-ai-chatbot-to-support-student-mental-health/

European Commission. (2024, August 1). European Artificial Intelligence Act comes into force [Press release]. https://ec.europa.eu/commission/presscorner/api/files/document/print/en/ip_24_4123/IP_24_4123_EN.pdf

Fitzpatrick, K. K., Darcy, A., & Vierhile, M. (2017). Delivering cognitive behavior therapy to young adults with symptoms of depression and anxiety using a fully automated conversational agent (Woebot): A randomized controlled trial. *JMIR Mental Health*, 4(2), e19–e19. https://doi.org/10.2196/mental.7785

Freeman, D., Reeve, S., Robinson, A., Ehlers, A., Clark, D., Spanlang, B., & Slater, M. (2017). Virtual reality in the assessment, understanding, and treatment of mental health disorders. *Psychological Medicine*, *47*(14), 2393–2400.

Graham, S., Depp, C., Lee, E. E. *et al.* (2019). Artificial intelligence for mental health and mental illnesses: An overview. *Current Psychiatry Reports*, *21*, 116. https://doi.org/10.1007/s11920-019-1094-0

Halbig, A., Babu, S. K., Gatter, S., Latoschik, M. E., Brukamp, K., & von Mammen, S. (2022). Opportunities and challenges of virtual reality in healthcare – A domain experts inquiry. *Frontiers in Virtual Reality*, *3*. https://doi.org/10.3389/frvir.2022.837616

Hassija, V., Chamola, V., Mahapatra, A., Singal, A., Goel, D., Huang, K., Scardapane, S., Spinelli, I., Mahmud, M., & Hussain, A. (2024). Interpreting black-box models: A review on explainable artificial intelligence. *Cognitive Computation*, *16*(1), 45–74. https://doi.org/10.1007/s12559-023-10179-8

Hollis, C., Falconer, C. J., Martin, J. L., Whittington, C., Stockton, S., Glazebrook, C., & Davies, E. B. (2017). Annual research review: Digital health interventions for children and young people with mental health problems – A systematic and meta-review. *Journal of Child Psychology and Psychiatry*, *58*(4), 474–503. https://doi.org/10.1111/jcpp.12663

Inkster, B., Sarda, S., & Subramanian, V. (2018). An empathy-driven, conversational artificial intelligence agent (Wysa) for digital mental well-being: Real-world data evaluation mixed-methods study. *JMIR mHealth and uHealth*, *6*(11), e12106. https://doi.org/10.2196/12106

Iqbal, A. I., Aamir, A., Hammad, A., Hafsa, H., Basit, A., Oduoye, M. O., Anis, M. W., Ahmed, S., Younus, M. I., & Jabeen, S. (2024). [Rev. of immersive technologies in healthcare: An in-depth exploration of virtual reality and augmented reality in enhancing patient care, medical education, and training paradigms]. *Journal of Primary Care & Community Health*, *15*, 21501319241293311. https://doi.org/10.1177/21501319241293311

Kim, M., Yoo, S., & Kim, C. (2022). Miniaturization for wearable EEG systems: Recording hardware and data processing. *Biomedical Engineering Letters*, *12*(3), 239–250. https://doi.org/10.1007/s13534-022-00232-0

Kiss, J., Edwards, G., Bouserhal, Rachel, Champagne, E., Belleguic, T., Psyché, V., Batcho, C., Hudon, C., Ratté, S., Verdruyckt, I., Parizeau, M.-H., Liu-Rosenbaum, A., Hudson, J., Bourbeau, M.-L., Lemieux, M., & Charbonneau, A. (2023). Harnessing artificial intelligence for early and evolution of Alzheimer's disease detections and enhancing senior mental health through innovative art-singing therapies: A multidisciplinary approach. *Faculty Scholarship*, *486*. https://digitalcommons.lindenwood.edu/faculty-research-papers/486

Luxton, D. D. (Ed.). (2016). *Artificial Intelligence in Behavioral and Mental Health Care*. Elsevier Academic Press. https://doi.org/10.1016/B978-0-12-420248-1.00001-5

Maita, K. C., Maniaci, M. J., Haider, C. R., Avila, F. R., Torres-Guzman, R. A., Borna, S., Lunde, J. J., Coffey, J. D., Demaerschalk, B. M., & Forte, A. J. (2024). The Impact of Digital Health Solutions on Bridging the Health Care Gap in Rural Areas: A Scoping Review. *The Permanente Journal*, 28(3), 130–143. https://doi.org/10.7812/TPP/23.134

Miner, A. S., Milstein, A., & Hancock, J. T. (2017). Talking to machines about personal mental health problems. *JAMA: The Journal of the American Medical Association*, *318*(13), 1217–1218. https://doi.org/10.1001/jama.2017.14151

Nath, R. K., & Thapliyal, H. (2021). Machine learning-based anxiety detection in older adults using wristband sensors and context feature. *SN Computer Science*, *2*(5), 359. https://doi.org/10.1007/s42979-021-00744-z

Ni, Y., & Jia, F. (2025). A scoping review of AI-driven digital interventions in mental health care: Mapping applications across screening, support, monitoring, prevention, and clinical education. *Healthcare (Basel, Switzerland)*, *13*(10), 1205. https://doi.org/10.3390/healthcare13101205

Olawade, D. B., Wada, O. Z., Odetayo, A., David-Olawade, A. C., Asaolu, F., & Eberhardt, J. (2024). Enhancing mental health with artificial intelligence: Current trends and future prospects. *Journal of Medicine, Surgery, and Public Health*, *3*, 100099. https://doi.org/10.1016/j.glmedi.2024.100099

Organisation for Economic Co-operation and Development. (2024, May 3). OECD updates AI Principles to stay abreast of rapid technological developments [Press release]. https://www.oecd.org/en/about/news/press-releases/2024/05/oecd-updates-ai-principles-to-stay-abreast-of-rapid-technological-developments.html

Pham T. (2025). Ethical and legal considerations in healthcare AI: Innovation and policy for safe and fair use. *Royal Society Open Science*, *12*(5), 241873. https://doi.org/10.1098/rsos.241873

Reece, A. G., Reagan, A. J., Lix, K. L. M., Dodds, P. S., Danforth, C. M., & Langer, E. J. (2017). Forecasting the onset and course of mental illness with Twitter data. *Scientific Reports*, *7*, 13006. https://doi.org/10.1038/s41598-017-12961-9

Sehgal, N. K. R., Kambhamettu, H., Matam, S. P., Ungar, L., & Guntuku, S. C. (2025). *Exploring socio-cultural challenges and opportunities in designing mental health chatbots for adolescents in India*. https://doi.org/10.48550/arxiv.2503.08562

Shatte, A. B. R., Hutchinson, D. M., & Teague, S. J. (2019). Machine learning in mental health: A scoping review of methods and applications. *Psychological Medicine*, *49*(9), 1426–1448.

Siddals, S., Torous, J., & Coxon, A. (2024). *"It happened to be the perfect thing"*: Experiences of generative AI chatbots for mental health. *npj Mental Health Research*, *3*, 48. https://doi.org/10.1038/s44184-024-00097-4

Song, T., Jamieson, J., Zhu, T., Yamashita, N., & Lee, Y.-C. (2025). *From interaction to attitude: Exploring the impact of human-AI cooperation on mental illness stigma*. https://doi.org/10.48550/arxiv.2501.01220

Tavory, T. (2024). Regulating AI in mental health: Ethics of care perspective. *JMIR Mental Health*, *11*, e58493. https://doi.org/10.2196/58493

Thakkar, A., Gupta, A., & De Sousa, A. (2024). Artificial intelligence in positive mental health: A narrative review. *Frontiers in Digital Health*, *6*, 1280235. https://doi.org/10.3389/fdgth.2024.1280235

Timmons, A. C., Duong, J. B., Simo Fiallo, N., Lee, T., Vo, H. P. Q., Ahle, M. W., Comer, J. S., Brewer, L. C., Frazier, S. L., & Chaspari, T. (2023).

A call to action on assessing and mitigating bias in artificial Intelligence applications for mental health. *Perspectives on Psychological Science*, *18*(5), 1062–1096. https://doi.org/10.1177/17456916221134490

Tulk Jesso, S., Kelliher, A., Sanghavi, H., Martin, T., & Henrickson Parker, S. (2022). Inclusion of clinicians in the development and evaluation of clinical artificial intelligence tools: A systematic literature review. *Frontiers in Psychology*, *13*, 830345–830345. https://doi.org/10.3389/fpsyg.2022.830345

UK Parliamentary (2025). *AI and mental healthcare: Ethical and regulatory considerations* (POSTnote No. 738). UK Parliament. https://researchbriefings.files.parliament.uk/documents/POST-PN-0738/POST-PN-0738.pdf

University of Washington. (2024, October 9). *Initiative-Funded Project Studies How Culturally Sensitive Communication Styles Affect Health AI*. Population Health. https://www.washington.edu/populationhealth/2024/10/09/initiative-funded-project-studies-how-culturally-sensitive-communication-styles-affects-health-ai

Yim, S. J., Lui, L. M. W., Lee, Y., Rosenblat, J. D., Ragguett, R.-M., Park, C., Subramaniapillai, M., Cao, B., Zhou, A., Rong, C., Lin, K., Ho, R. C., Coles, A. S., Majeed, A., Wong, E. R., Phan, L., Nasri, F., & McIntyre, R. S. (2020). The utility of smartphone-based, ecological momentary assessment for depressive symptoms. *Journal of Affective Disorders*, *274*, 602–609. https://doi.org/10.1016/j.jad.2020.05.116

Yong, E., Teo, Y. N., & Yong, K. H. (2025). AI technology: A new game changer for the future mental health industry? *Asia-Pacific Journal of Public Health*, *37*(1), 148–149. https://doi.org/10.1177/10105395241303790

Zidaru, T., Morrow, E. M., & Stockley, R. (2021). Ensuring patient and public involvement in the transition to AI-assisted mental health care: A systematic scoping review and agenda for design justice. *Health Expectations: An International Journal of Public Participation in Health Care and Health Policy*, *24*(4), 1072–1124. https://doi.org/10.1111/hex.13299

Index

Pages in *italics* refer to figures and pages in **bold** refer to tables.

For Product Safety Concerns and Information please contact our EU representative GPSR@taylorandfrancis.com Taylor & Francis Verlag GmbH, Kaufingerstraße 24, 80331 München, Germany